88 Plus! PAPER CAPERS

By Muriel Hemmings

STANDARD
PUBLISHING

Cincinnati, Ohio

The Standard Publishing Company, Cincinnati, Ohio
A division of Standex International Corporation

00 99 98 97 96 95 94 93   5 4 3 2 1

ISBN 0-87403-739-5

Read Me First!

Every item in this book can be made from a piece of typing paper. This inexpensive, plain white paper will allow children to color and decorate their crafts as they choose, but you may also wish to experiment with colored copy-machine paper, origami paper, and gift-wrapping paper. Another paper that works surprisingly well, especially for accordion-folded things (fan, page 48, butterflies, page 26) is a page from a catalog with colored printing on both sides. Construction paper does not fold easily, but may work for some of the more simple crafts.

Many of the crafts begin with a square of paper. Rather than take up space throughout the book showing how to make a square from a piece of typing paper, the instructions are shown here only.

Fold one corner of the paper down, creating a triangle, and align the edges as perfectly as possible. Fold or draw a line along the paper extending past the triangle, and cut this piece off.

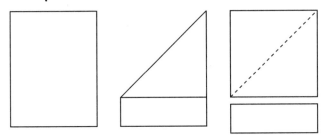

Rather than start a craft with a piece of paper that has a fold through the center, you may wish to simply remember that by cutting 2 1/2 inches off one end of a piece of typing paper, you will be left with an 8 1/2 inch square. This will be even easier to do (especially in mass quantities) with a paper cutter.

Some crafts will hold up longer if two layers of typing paper are used. You may also wish to let children color the craft on one piece of typing paper and then glue it to another sheet before finishing the craft. This will not only make the finished product more sturdy, but will also allow the use of felt markers, since the color that bleeds through will be covered up by the second sheet.

Very few crafts will call for items that may not be readily available in your classroom; a pair of needle-nose pliers for example. But be sure to carefully read through the instructions before class time to make sure you have what you need. Pupils will need strong, sharp scissors for many of the paper capers.

Most paper capers can be made by third and fourth graders. First and second graders who can use scissors well will need adult guidance. To help you select capers, the following scale has been devised:

●   Easy

▲   Moderately Easy

■   Requires Some Help

★   Requires Good Dexterity

Contents

Impossible Paper Capers

When the Lord Jesus lived on earth He did wonderful things that you or I could never do. Often, by simply speaking the words, He made sick people well, blind people see, deaf people hear, lame people walk, even dead people come alive again. He can perform these miracles because He is really God, who created everything in the first place. We cannot perform miracles, but we can do some things with paper that seem impossible. For example, did you know you can walk through a half of a piece of paper? Let's try!

Walk Through a Paper

1. Fold and cut a sheet of paper in half.

2. Color one of the halves or leave it white.

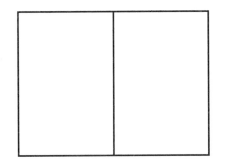

3. Fold a half in half lengthwise. Cut slits about inch apart almost to the fold.

4. Turn the paper around and from the folded edge, cut slits between the first slits, not quite to the outside edge.

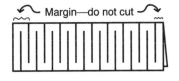

Margin—do not cut

5. Now cut along the fold, leaving an uncut margin on each end.

6. Open the paper and walk through it.

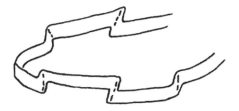

Paper Mystery

1. Cut a one-inch strip from a sheet of paper.

2. Make a twist in the strip and tape the ends together.

3. Cut completely around the center of the strip of paper.

4. You will have two links of a chain mysteriously joined together!

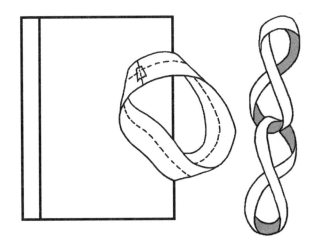

Tiny Town

Houses supply us with shelter from bad weather and comfortable places to live. When God created our world He gave us wood, stone, material to make bricks, and everything else we need to build a house. Did you know that paper wasps also use wood to build their hives? They chew tiny pieces of wood until it is wet and gooey—like paper wads get when you chew them! Then the wasps use this gooey paper to build strong, light, and warm houses! As a matter of fact, people may have learned the secret of making paper by watching these wasps. Let's make a paper house, or even a town, for tiny paper friends.

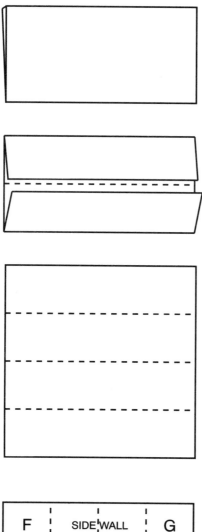

A House

1. Start with a square. Fold the square in half and press the crease (A).

2. Open the square and fold the bottom of the paper up to the center crease. Do the same with the top (B).

3. Open the square, which now has four sections. Turn the paper and make these same three folds again from the other direction, so that you are left with a paper that is divided into sixteen small squares (C).

4. Mark the six heavy lines indicated and cut them (D).

5. To build your house, place square A over square B and square C over square D. Before gluing, make note of how the roof peaks and where the door and windows will be. Mark these lightly in pencil.

6. Now lay the paper flat to color the roof, doors and windows, and whatever else you desire (shrubs, drain pipes, etc.). Very young children will find it even easier to color these features before the

heavy lines are cut. Or, they may draw windows, shrubs, etc. on another piece of paper, cut them out and glue them onto the house after it is formed.

7. Build your house. Glue square A over square B and square C over square D to form the peaked roof. To form the walls, glue E and F over C/D and G and H over A/B.

8. Cut a door. If you would like a chimney, fold a scrap of paper in four sections, cut out the two vee shapes indicated, tape or glue side A to side B and tape or glue the chimney to the roof.

9. A porch may be made from a piece of paper 2 inches long and 1 inch wide. Fold and cut on heavy lines. Fold and glue A and B under E, and fold and glue D and C under F.

10. For a larger house, make two houses and glue them together in various positions. For a smaller section of the house and/or a garage, start with a smaller square.

For a modern city you could build skyscrapers by stacking several Bible-times houses (page 12) on top of each other. (You could use the stairs as a fire escape or leave them off.) Glue several of these houses together, one on top of another and side-by-side for a big department store. Draw large display windows.

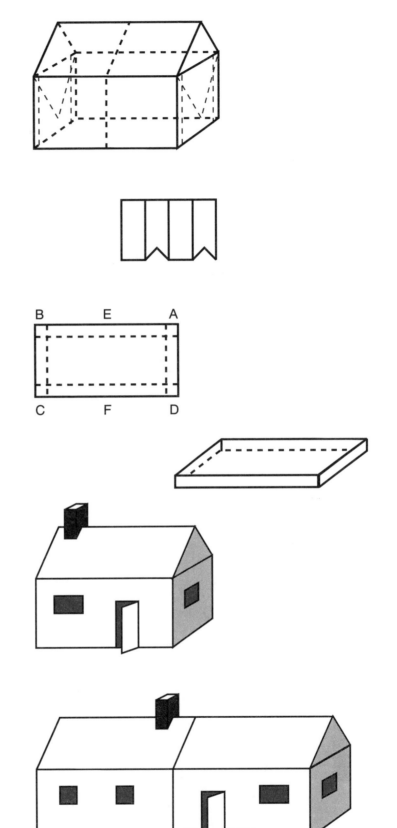

In Sunday school and church we learn about the Lord Jesus who is really God himself. Jesus came to earth and lived like we do so that He (and God) would know exactly what it is like to be human. Another reason God wanted to be one of us for a while was so He could explain His plans and help us understand them better. We go to Sunday school and church to worship God, to learn more about Him, and to study His plans for us found in the Bible.

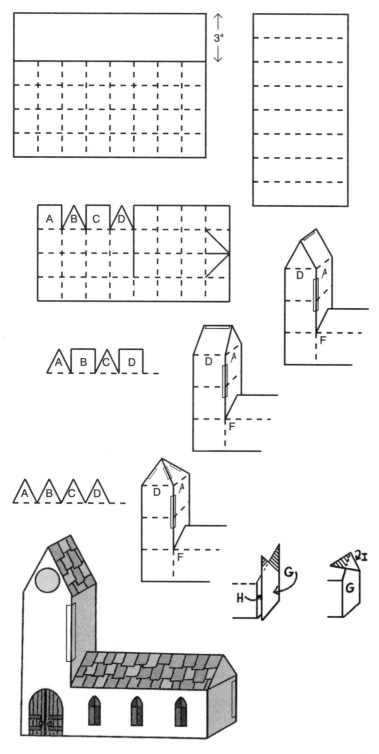

A Church With a Steeple

1. Measure and cut three inches off the long side of a piece of paper. Fold the remaining sheet of paper in half. Open and fold each half in half. Fold each of these two sections in half, so that you have eight strips.

2. Open the paper. Fold into fourths in the other direction. Open the paper. You should have thirty-two sections.

3. Mark the heavy lines indicated and cut.

4. To see where to color the steeple, roof, windows, doors, and whatever other features you want, fold the church as described in steps 6 and 7. Then open the paper to color it. (You may color stained-glass windows and doors separately and add them after church is assembled.)

5. Alternate steeple roof styles are shown. Cut to make the style you prefer. To make the steeple, fold sides A and B over sides C and D and tape. Open and tape along top edge of steeple roof.

6. Now form your church by folding back at center of roof and taping side E to steeple side B. Fold end G over H and tape. Cut off excess paper at peak. Fold I over J and cut excess paper at roof line. Do same for J. Tape ends to roof. Cut or paste door here or on steeple end or on steeple side.

Skyscraper
or Apartment Building

1. Fold a piece of paper into fourths. Open. Measure 1 1/2 inches from the top, draw a line across the page, and fold along this line.

2. Open this fold and cut along the heavy lines indicated, down to the fold. The paper above this fold will be the roof of your skyscraper.

3. Lay the paper flat. Color each of the four large sections to look like the sides of a tall building with many windows.

4. To form your skyscraper, fold the paper in half and tape A to D. Open the paper into a square and stand. Fold the top flaps in and tape or glue to form the roof.

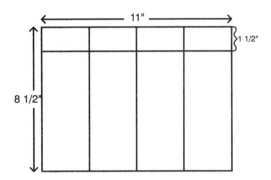

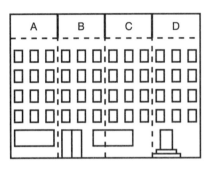

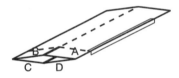

The Lord Jesus promised that all who love Him and accept Him as Savior will live in a mansion prepared especially for them. Jesus tells us in John 14:2, 3, and 6, "There are many rooms in my Father's house. I would not tell you this if it were not true. I am going there to prepare a place for you. After I go and prepare a place for you, I will come back. Then I will take you to be with me so that you may be where I am. I am the way. And I am the truth and the life. The only way to the Father is through me."

Following the instructions on the next page, let's make a heavenly mansion.

A Castle
or Heavenly Mansion

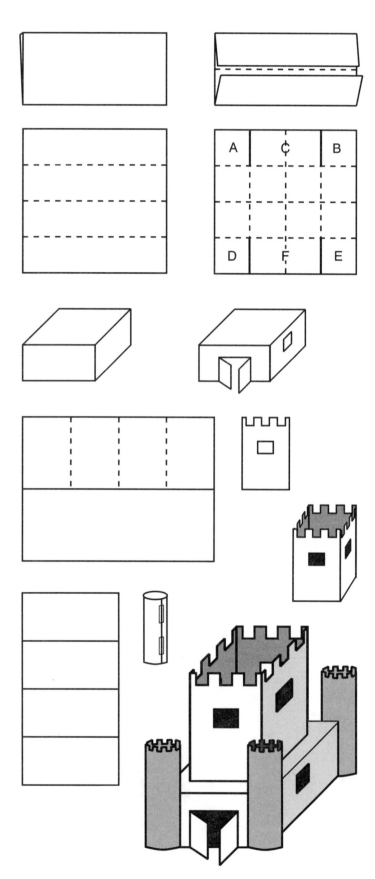

1. Start with a square. Fold the square in half and reopen. Fold the top down to the center crease. Fold the bottom up to the center crease. Open, and fold the same way from the other direction, making sixteen small squares.

2. Make the four cuts indicated by the heavy lines. Fold A and B inside C. Fold D and E inside F, to make a box. Note where doors, windows, bricks, etc. will go. Lay paper flat and color as you wish.

3. Cut the doorways and windows that you colored in the castle. To cut a square out of the top, measure 3/4 of an inch from each edge, draw a line, and cut. Then glue side flaps A and B inside C, and D and E inside F.

4. For the inside tower, fold and cut a sheet of paper in half lengthwise, and use one half. (Save the other.)

5. Fold into fourths. Mark position of windows, etc., lay paper flat and color it. Cut turrets and windows in this section.

6. Fold the paper in half and tape the two edges together. Then open into a square. Cut turrets in the top.

7. Place this square tower inside the hole you cut in the roof of the castle.

8. Use the remaining half sheet of paper to make the towers. Color one side. Fold and cut into fourths. Roll each piece into a tube and tape to close. Cut an odd number of turrets.

9. Glue or tape one of these towers at each corner of the castle.

14

A Bible-Times House

People who lived when Jesus did built houses with flat roofs. They used the tops of their houses as we use a porch or a patio. Sometimes they even built a little room up there for guests. Let's make a house like one where Jesus lived.

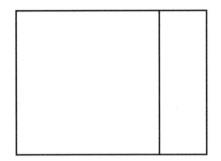

1. Start with a square. (Save the strip of paper you cut off when making the square.) Fold the square into sixteen squares. (See steps 1 through 3 from "A House" on page 10.)

2. The four center squares will be the roof. Color the building to look like it was made of clay bricks and/or stones. Draw flowers and pretty mats on the roof. Draw windows and doors on the sides. Cut the heavy lines indicated.

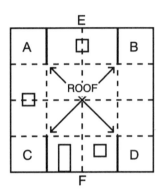

3. Fold and glue A and B under E, and C and D under F. Cut doors and windows.

4. Take the strip of paper you cut off to make your square. Fold and cut it in half lengthwise. Cut one of these pieces into four strips. Color these and glue them around the roof to form a railing.

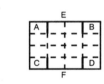

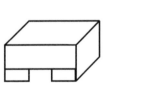

5. To add an "upper room" to your house, take the remaining piece of paper and fold it as you would to make a house (but don't cut it into a square first).

6. When you tape or glue A and B under E and C and D under F, you will notice that two sides of your little room are partly open. Glue one open side to the railing so that the opening is hidden. Use the other opening for your door.

7. Fold a strip of paper 3/4 inch wide and 5 1/4 inches long into steps and tape these steps to the side of your house.

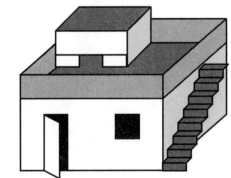

Trees

God made trees to be a shelter for birds and animals. Insects also need trees. Trees clean the air and make it safe to breathe. Can you think of more ways trees are useful to us?

Leafy Tree

1. Fold a sheet of paper into fourths.

2. Fold lengthwise in half. You now have eight layers.

3. Cut out half a tree along the fold, giving the trunk a wide base to help the tree stand. (To avoid having to cut through eight layers, children can trace the pattern several times and cut only two or fours layers at a time.)

4. Open your paper(s) and you should have four trees. Color the trees on one side.

5. Glue or tape the four plain sides together, half a tree at a time, meeting in the center so the the tree has four sides and stands by itself.

6. Draw a bird in a nest and glue it to the tree. Cut an opening in the base for a chipmunk's home.

Patterns for trees and bird nest are on page 86.

Palm Tree

1. Divide and cut a sheet of paper into fourths.

2. Color one of the four sections brown, roll it lengthwise into a cylinder, and tape it. Cut short slits at the bottom of this tree trunk.

3. Fold another section of the paper into eight parts. Glue or tape the eight layers together to form a stand for the tree. Color the top layer green (before you tape it).

4. Open the slits on the trunk and glue them to the base so the tree will stand.

5. Color two sections green on both sides (or use green paper). Fold and cut one piece into fourths and cut out branches as shown.

6. Fold and cut the last section in half. Fold each piece into fourths and cut out branches.

7. Open the three branches, apply glue, and gently push the center of each into the top of the trunk, sandwiching the large layer between the two smaller branches.

   This type of palm tree may have shaded the house where Jesus lived.

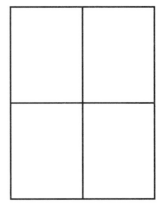

People, Animals, and Vehicles

Stand-Up People and Animals

Use strips of paper to make people, or animals, or vehicles. The size of each figure will be determined by the size of the strip you start with. You may cut a piece of paper into thirds or fourths, for example. To make animals shorter than people, fold your paper into sixths.

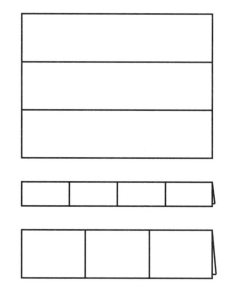

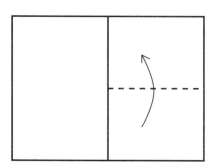

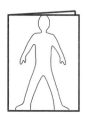

1. Divide your paper into strips, however wide you choose.

2. Fold a strip in half lengthwise.

3. Fold and cut the strip into four sections crosswise.

4. On each section, draw a car, truck, bus, dog, cat, etc. You may draw a small animal next to a large bus, just be sure to put the top of your item at the top of the paper, and leave a portion connected at the fold so that it will stand up. Color the items. When you cut them out, remember to leave them connected at the fold.

Another Way to Make Figures

1. Fold and cut a sheet of paper in half.

2. Fold one of the halves in half, draw your figure, and cut it out (you will have two).

3. Color one of the figures as the front, color the other as the back, and glue the two together.

18

A Line of Boys and Girls

1. Fold and cut a sheet of paper length-wise into fourths.

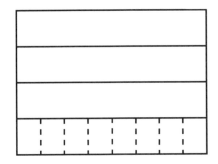

2. Fold a strip in half three times so you have eight sections.

3. Draw a half a boy and girl on the top section. Cut them out, open the paper, and cut off the half-person on each end.

4. Color your paper people. You could color them black, brown, yellow and pink to remind yourself that God made folks of different colors because He loves them that way.

Finger Puppets

1. Fold and cut a sheet of paper into fourths.

2. Fold and cut each quarter sheet into fourths.

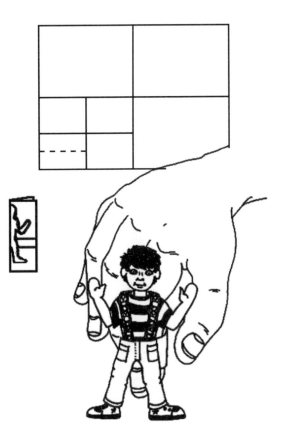

3. Fold each small piece of paper in half and cut out half a person or animal along the fold, leaving a tab on both sides.

4. Color the figure and tape around your finger, facing you or facing away. You could have a whole family on one hand visiting a family on the other hand. You can cut sixteen figures from one sheet of paper.

Transportation

When God created us, He gave us legs to help us walk from place to place. He also gave us the ability to invent faster ways of getting around. Let's start with an old form of transportation and move toward the modern.

A Covered Wagon and Horses

1. Fold and cut a sheet of paper in half. Fold one half in half lengthwise and draw two horses and a driver. Color them.

2. Cut out the horses, double, and glue them together with three inches of thread or string between them. Do not put glue on the legs.

3. Cut the driver out, double. Glue the front and back together to make him stronger. Cut a small strip off the scrap paper and roll it up for a seat, or make a bench by folding a strip as shown.

4. For the pioneers' wagon, fold and cut a sheet of paper into four pieces as shown in the diagram.

5. Fold A in half and glue together to make it more firm.

6. Color one side like a pretty blanket as this is inside the wagon. Raise each side a little, and crease.

7. Color C and glue each end to the inside of the raised part.

8. Add four wheels cut from B.

9. Glue the seat at the front of the wagon. Glue the driver in a sitting position on the seat.

10. Attach the other ends of the horses' strings to the driver or the inside of the wagon.

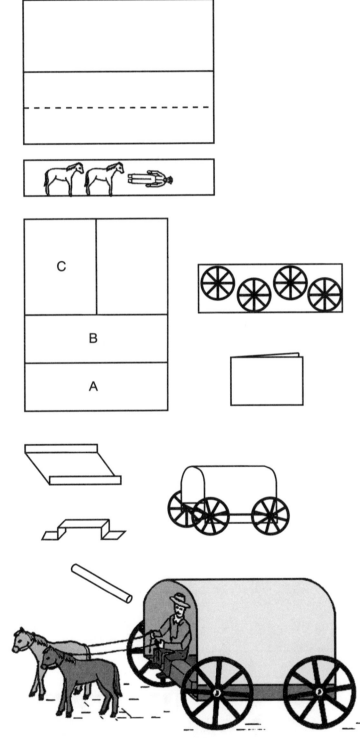

Patterns are on page 87.

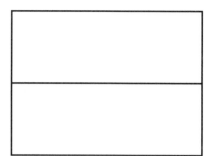

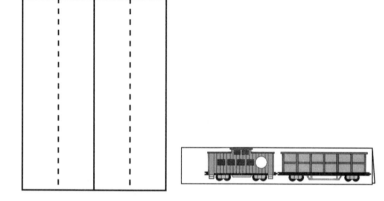

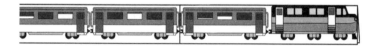

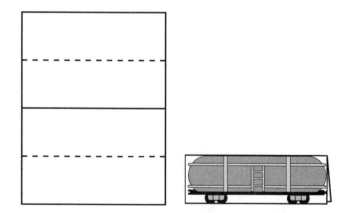

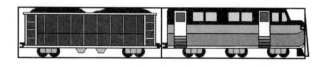

Cars and Trucks

1. Fold and cut a sheet of paper in half lengthwise.

2. Fold one piece in half lengthwise and draw cars, trucks, and buses on it. Make sure that your vehicles reach the top fold (leave extra space at the bottom for shorter vehicles).

3. Color them and cut them out double, leaving the fold so they can stand by themselves.

A Train

1. Fold and cut a sheet of paper in half.

2. Fold each piece lengthwise.

3. Draw the engine and about three coaches on one piece and four coaches on the other piece, along the fold at the top.

4. Color and cut out, double, leaving a piece connected at the top fold.

5. Tape the train cars together. They should stand by themselves when the wheels are spread out.

These instructions make a train in the correct proportions to the rest of Tiny Town. If you care more that the activity be easier, fold and cut a piece of paper in half, then fold each half in half for each train car. Patterns for this size are on pages 88, 89.

The Rocket

1. Fold and cut a sheet of paper in half. Color one side of one half.

2. Roll it to a point at the top (to form a cone) and tape it.

3. Cut the bottom so it is even.

4. For the rocket base, fold and cut the other piece of paper in half.

5. Fold and cut a square. Color it.

6. Fold the square point to point.

7. Fold this triangle in half.

8. Cut a small triangle off the top. Fold the remaining strip in half to form the creases you will need to fit inside the rocket.

9. Open your paper and it should look something like this. Pinch the base together until it looks like figure X.

10. Cut four evenly spaced slits in the cone bottom.

11. Set these slits on the four creases of the base.

12. Color the remaining strip of paper to look like fire. Fold and cut into fourths and cut a fringe. Glue each 1/4 section under rocket cone between base stands.

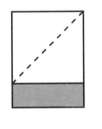
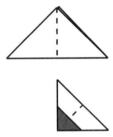
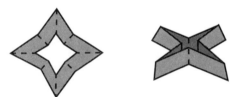
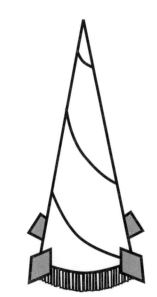

Doll House People and Furniture

Lori and Kevin gazed through the window at the pelting rain. There was nothing good on TV, and every game in the house had been played.

"Oh, why does it have to rain on Saturdays?" Kevin moaned.

"Would you rather live in a desert where nothing grows but cactus?" Lori asked him.

"And live on cactus juice? No way!" Kevin shuddered.

"Then we should be thankful that God sends rain, even on Saturdays," Lori said. Suddenly, she jumped to her feet. "I know what we can do! Let's look in the basement for a big box and make it into a doll's house!"

"Cool!" said Kevin. "I'll make the furniture!"

A Boy and a Girl

1. Fold and cut a sheet of paper in half.

2. Fold one piece in half twice, lengthwise, so you have four layers.

3. Fold in half crosswise so you have eight layers. Draw a boy without arms. His head should reach the top fold. Color both sides. Cut out the eight-layer thick boy, leaving his head connected at the top. (It will be easier to cut if you open the top fold and cut four layers at a time.)

4. Use the remaining half sheet of paper for the arms. Fold and cut it in half. Fold one small piece twice as you did for the body.

5. Cut around the arms, color, and slip between folds of shirt. Add a drop of glue to keep arms in place.

6. If you wish, fold the remaining quarter section in four layers, glue the layers together, and tape the boy's feet to this platform to make him more stable.

7. Make a girl in the same way. Give her long hair and glue a skirt to her waist, if you like.

Patterns are on page 90.

24

Pets

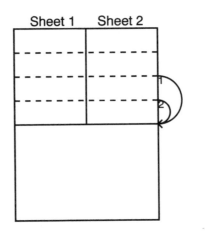

1. Fold and cut a paper into fourths.

2. Fold one of the fourths in half twice so you have four layers.

3. Draw and cut out the head, body, tail (or a tail can be made from scrap paper). Color both sides and add a face.

4. Cut and color ears and glue them to the side of the head.

Patterns for ears—full size

5. Fold another quarter of the sheet so you have four layers. Fold this in half lengthwise and outline, color and cut out the pet's legs.

6. Glue a set of legs either over or inside the front of the body and a set over the rear. Spread the four legs at the base so the animal can stand by itself.

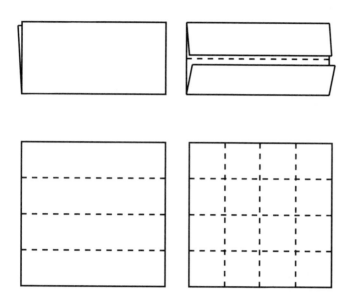

Furniture

1. For all of the furniture, start with a square.

2. Fold the square in half, open. Fold the top edge down to the center crease. Fold the bottom edge up to the center crease, making four sections.

3. Open the paper and repeat steps one and two from the other direction and you will have sixteen small squares. Continue from this point to make each piece.

A Square Table and a Long Table

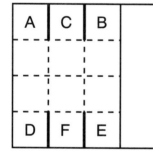

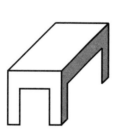

1. Start with the paper folded into sixteen squares. Color one side.

2. For a square table, make four cuts indicated by the heavy lines.

3. Glue or tape A and B behind C.

4. Glue or tape E and D behind F.

5. You have an upside down basket. Cut the four corners into table legs.

6. For a long, narrow table, cut off one row of squares, leaving twelve. Color it and follow directions for the square table.

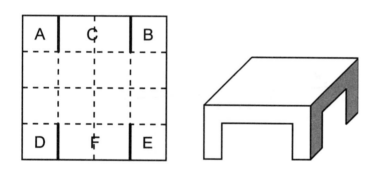

Coffee Table

1. Follow the directions above for the long table, then cut the legs short.

A Bed

1 Start with the square folded into sixteen squares. Trim off one row of squares so that you are left with twelve.

2. Fold each of the outside ten squares into half sections, so the bed will be half as high as the table. Tape or glue under.

3. Cut the four lines indicated. Fold A and B behind C. Tape and glue.

4. Fold D and E behind F. Tape or glue.

5. Cut a head board and foot board and glue in place.

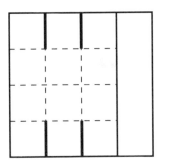

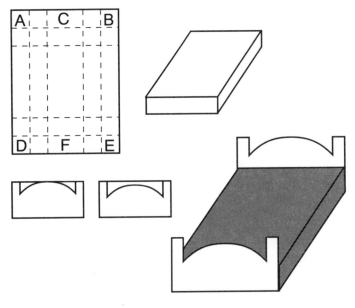

A Sofa

1. Follow directions for making the bed but color the paper to look like a pretty sofa.

2. Take the four small squares you cut off. Fold in half and cut along the fold for a sofa back. Decorate like the sofa and glue in place for back and arms.

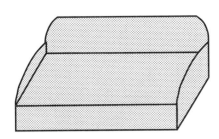

A Refrigerator or a Dresser

1. Follow directions for the bed.

2. Turn it upright and draw or cut out a door.

3. Turn it sideways and draw drawers for a dresser.

A Stove

1. Follow directions for a square table.

2. Draw the burners and oven. Glue a narrow paper strip to the back.

An End Table

1. Fold and cut a sheet of paper into fourths. Make a square from one fourth.

3. Follow directions for making the square table.

A Chair

1. Follow directions for making the end table.

2. Cut a chair back to fit and glue it to the back of the table.

A Cradle

1. Fold and cut a sheet of paper into fourths. Make a square from one fourth. Fold into sixteen small squares and cut off a row of four squares, leaving twelve.

2. Color in a pastel shade. Make the four cuts indicated. Glue A and B behind C. Glue D and E behind F.

3. Turn open side up. Cut out two rockers and glue to the ends.

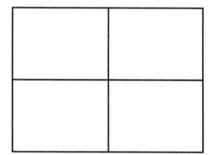

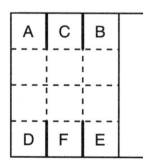

Why Did God Do That?

You probably know about the fish that swallowed Jonah and then spit him out onto dry land three days later. Why did God send a fish to swallow Jonah? And why was Jonah thrown overboard? And why did God send the big storm? If you're not sure about the answers to these questions, read Jonah's book in the Bible. After you've read it, think about these questions

Do you think that God was giving Jonah a second chance? What might God have done instead to punish Jonah for his disobedience?

Have you ever been saved from punishment that you deserved because someone decided to give you a second chance? Have you ever disobeyed God? How many chances does God give you to do the right thing?

As you make this paper caper, think about the many times God allows you to try again. He never says, "That's it! I'm not going to forgive you anymore!" Let's thank God for giving us new opportunities every day to try and be better people, and let's think of this paper caper as a special reminder that God is good, and patient, and always gives us another chance.

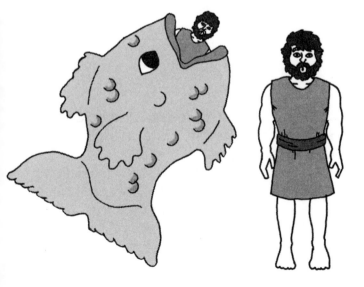

Jonah and the Big Fish

1. Fold a piece of paper into fourths.

2. From these four layers, cut a fat fish with the tail at the fold. You will have two double fish. (Pattern on page 91.)

3. Take one double fish and cut two slits (about an inch apart) from the fold half way to the mouth.

4. Open the fish and pull the tab to the inside.

5. Using another piece of paper, draw, color, and cut out a 2 to 3-inch tall Jonah. (Pattern on page 91.) Glue or tape him to the tab you have just created.

6. Color the outside of the other fish and glue it over the fish that contains Jonah. Help Jonah pop in and out of the fish's mouth.

Jacob's Dream

In Genesis 28, you will find an amazing story about a man named Jacob. He was hiding from his brother, he went to sleep using a rock a pillow, and he an a wonderful dream! Read the story and then follow the instructions to make the things that appear in the story. Then you can use your things to tell the story to a friend.

The Ladder

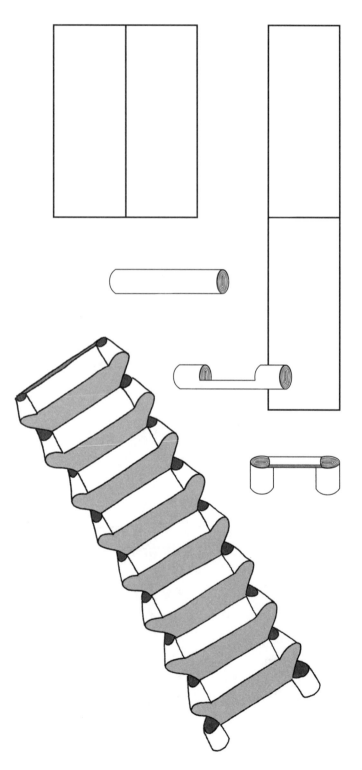

1. Fold and cut a sheet of paper in half.

2. Tape the two pieces end to end, making a long strip.

3. Roll the strip into a cylinder and tape.

4. With strong scissors, cut a chunk of paper out of the roll on the opposite side of the tape. Be careful not to cut clear through the roll.

5. With the taped edge down, bend the two ends of the roll under until it stands upright on a solid surface.

6. Gently pull the center upward and your paper will magically form a ladder!

Draw a picture of Heaven and color it as beautifully as you can. Glue this picture to the top of the ladder.

To make Jacob, follow the instructions on pages 18 or 24. Now you can crumple a piece of paper to make the rock that Jacob used for a pillow. To make stars and the angels, follow the directions on the next three pages.

The Angels

1. Use a compass or trace around an object to make a circle about five inches across. You will get three or four circles from one sheet of paper. Each circle will become an angel.

2. Cut out the circles and fold each in half. Draw half an angel, and cut it out.

3. Open your angel. Bend the wings back and the arms forward. Taper the arms into hands.

Now that you know how, you may make angels of all different sizes. Make some out of aluminum foil and paper doilies. Wouldn't these make pretty Christmas decorations?

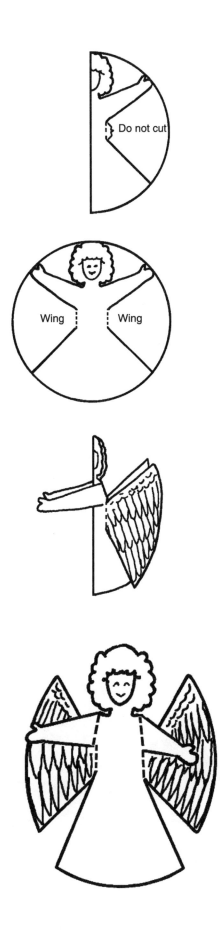

The Star of Bethlehem

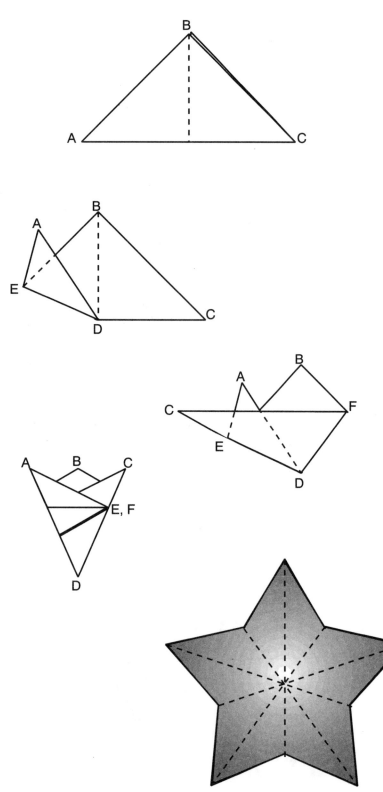

1. Start with a square. Fold and cut the square into fourths.

2. Color both sides.

3. Fold a square into a triangle, then fold the triangle in half to find the center, and open it.

4. Hold the center fold line with the thumb of your right hand and with your left hand, fold the left bottom up to a point in the middle of the left side.

5. Now fold BC over until its bottom aligns with the new bottom you just created.

6. Now fold AC back toward the right, until all the right edges align.

7. Starting at a point midway down the bottom triangle, cut up to the top right corner of that same triangle (indicated by the heavy line). Open your paper to find a perfect five-point star.

A Two-Dimensional Star

1. Color and cut two stars as described on the previous page.

2. Slit each star from one point to the center and slide them together.

3. Look at your finished star and note that one slit is pointing up and one is pointing down. Attach a thread to the right or the left of the slit pointing up. (If you put your thread in the wrong star, one will fall off when you try to hang it.)

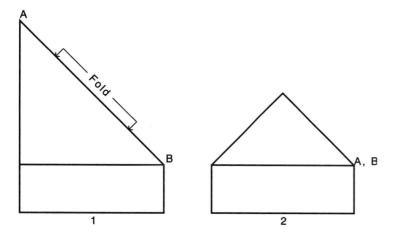

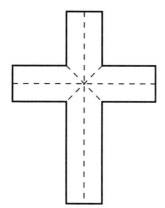

A Cross

When we see a cross we are reminded of the big wooden cross where the soldiers nailed the Lord Jesus. He accepted this torture willingly because He loves you and me enough to take the punishment we deserve for our sins. When we are sorry for the wrong we have done and ask Jesus to forgive us, He does. He will also guide us through the problems of this life and give us everlasting life in Heaven. Make a cross to remind you of all that Jesus has done for you.

1. Fold a sheet of paper as you would to get a square, but do not cut the strip off.

2. Fold A to B so it looks like figure 2.

3. Fold in half so it looks like figure 3.

4. Fold in half again. (Both sides are shown in figure 4.)

5. Cut a straight line right up the center.

6. Open the paper and discard the scraps; there is your cross.

You Are the Light of the World

Lamps, candles, and lanterns remind us that God wants us to be light for Him. How can you be God's light? Just let others know the Lord Jesus loves them, and show them the way to Him. God asks us to share His good news with others by inviting them to Sunday school, and by telling them how God helps us every day.

A Lantern

1. Fold and cut a sheet of paper in half.

2. Color one piece brilliantly on both sides.

3. Fold in half and cut slits about one-quarter inch apart up to about 1/2 inch from the edges of the paper.

4. Open the paper and tape the ends of the lantern together.

5. Color a strip of paper for a handle and fasten it to the lantern.

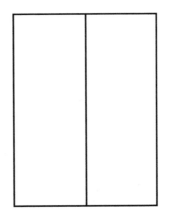

Small Lantern

1. Fold and cut a sheet of paper into fourths.

2. Take one piece and follow the directions above for a lantern.

Reversible Mask

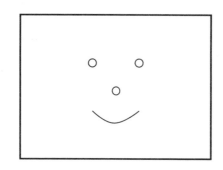

1. Use two sheets of paper and make a mask with each.

2. Hold a sheet of paper up to your face and mark with a pencil the location of your eyes, nose and mouth.

3. Fold the paper in half and cut these holes out, then cut the outline of the mask in any shape you wish—animal, giant, etc. Leave a tab on each side.

4. Make a different mask with another sheet of paper. Cut it out, leaving a tab on each side. Color both masks and join them by taping the tabs together to fit your head. Now you can be disguised coming and going.

Remember that it is all right to pretend to be someone or something else just for fun. But sometimes girls and boys claim to love the Lord Jesus, yet they forget to be kind to the boy down the street or to the shy girl who needs a friend. That is like wearing an "I love Jesus" mask on top of an "I don't care about pleasing Jesus" face.

A Surprise Christmas Cube

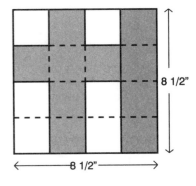

1. Fold a sheet of paper into fourths lengthwise, and into thirds widthwise OR,

1A. Fold a sheet of paper into sixteen squares as you did for making a basket and cut off one row of four squares.

2. Cut out a cross as indicated by the shaded area.

3. Print "GOD'S SON" on the squares.

4. Turn the cross over and decorate it with Christmas symbols, or however you like.

5. Form into a cube, with the decorated paper on the outside. Tape the edges together.

Now you have a cube that looks like a Christmas gift but has a secret inside. You can open your gift and explain to your friends that God's Son, Jesus, is the reason we celebrate Christmas. God's gift of Jesus is the greatest gift we will ever receive.

Blocks for Building

You can make and decorate more cubes (of any size) to use as building blocks. Why not make some for your younger brothers or sisters to play with? They will enjoy the blocks all the more because you made them.

Water Toys

A Fishing Net

1. Fold and cut a sheet of paper into fourths. Each fourth will become a net. (For a very large net, use a whole piece of paper.)

2. Fold one of the fourths in half. Then fold it again in the same direction.

3. Cut slits from one folded edge about 1/2 inch apart stopping 1/4 inch from the fold on the other side of the paper. Turn the paper around and cut slits between you first slits, again stopping 1/4 inch from the fold. (If you use lined notebook paper for this caper, the lines make good cutting guides.)

4. Carefully unfold, then open your net. Fill your net with colorful fish cut from scraps.

When Jesus saw Simon and Andrew throwing their nets into the lake, he said to them, "Come and follow me. I will make you fishermen for men." He meant that He would teach them how to teach others about God. Can you be a fisher of men?

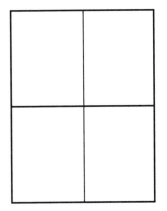

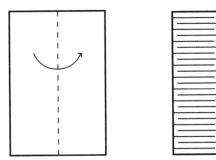

Let's make a boat like the one Jesus and His disciples might have been in when they were caught in a storm on the Sea of Galilee. Wild waves crashed over the little boat but as soon as Jesus said, "Peace, be still!" the waves calmed right down. Jesus could do this because He is a part of God and was present when everything was created in the first place. Because Jesus took part in the creation, He is able to control all of creation and is able to repair anything that goes wrong.

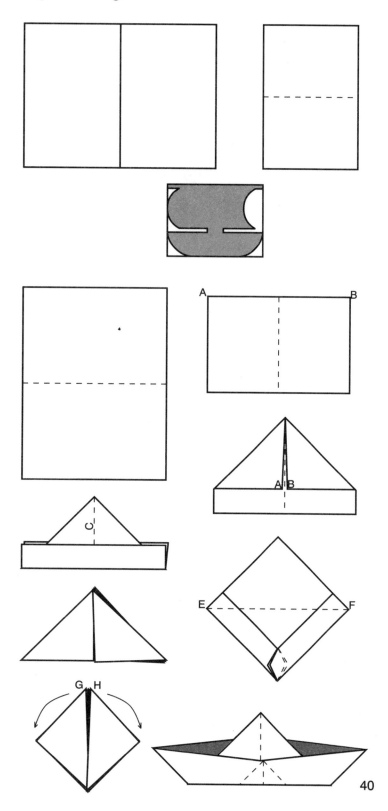

A Bible-Times Ship

1. Fold and cut a sheet of paper in half.

2. Fold one of the halves in half. Draw a boat, letting the sail extend to the fold at the top. Cut your boat out, being careful not to cut it apart at the top. (The fold is what holds your boat together.)

3. Color your ship on both sides. Spread the base so it will stand.

A Boat That Will Float

1. Fold a sheet of paper in half. Fold in half the other way to find the center. Open the last fold only.

2. With the fold on top, fold the two top corners down until they meet along the center.

3. Fold the strip along the bottom up, one on each side.

4. Slip thumbs inside, spread the paper apart, and refold into a square. (Tuck the strips inside each other.)

5. Fold each side up along E/F, bringing points up on opposite sides.

6. Slip thumbs inside, spread and fold into a new square.

7. With the folds facing your hands, pull gently on points G and H and you have a boat. Color it if you like. Try it on water.

40

A Drinking Cup

1. Start with a square. Fold it in half point to point to form a triangle.

2. Fold corner A over to B, making the top exactly horizontal to the base.

3. Fold corner C over to D, aligning with the top just made.

4. Fold the two points at the top down, one on each side.

5. Open the cup by pressing the sides. Fill with water and have a drink.

You may also use your cup as a game. Tape one end of a 12-inch string to the outside of the cup. Tape the other end to a crumpled piece of paper. See how long it takes to plop the paper ball into the cup.

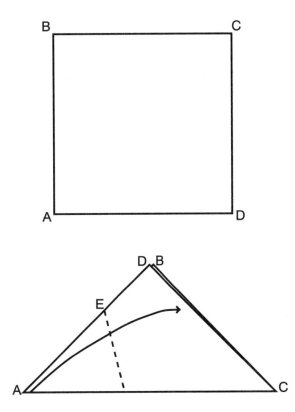

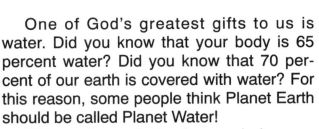

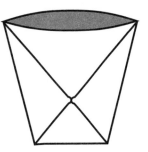

One of God's greatest gifts to us is water. Did you know that your body is 65 percent water? Did you know that 70 percent of our earth is covered with water? For this reason, some people think Planet Earth should be called Planet Water!

Did you know that a human being can live for as long as two months without food, but will die after only ten days without water?

Drinking water is one of the best things you can do to keep yourself healthy. You get some water when you eat or drink anything, but drinks that contain sugar will not quench your thirst as well as plain water. Remember this on a hot summer day when you are really thirsty!

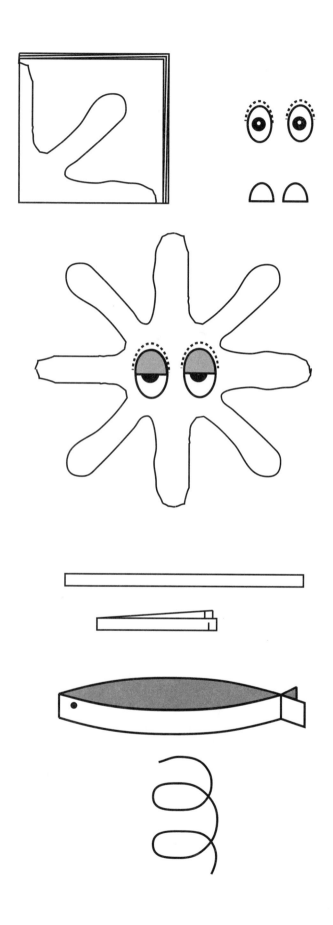

A Sleepy Octopus

1. Start with a square. Fold the square into fourths and cut as shown (Do not stretch the middle arm into the corner, or the tentacles will be different lengths.)

2. Open the eight-armed octopus.

3. Draw oval shapes with dark spots for eyes.

4. Cut around the top half of each eye and fold down to cover the bottom half.

5. Color both sides of the octopus except the eyes.

6. Close the eyes on your octopus and fold up the arms. Place him on a dish of water and watch him wake up!

Patterns are on page 92.

A Roly-Poly Fish

1. From any scrap, cut a strip of paper about 3/4-inch wide and as long as you want it. (The longer the strip, the bigger the fish.) Or use another sheet of paper and cut a whole school of fish, either lengthwise or crosswise. Color both sides of your strips.

2. About 1/2 inch from one end, cut a slit half way up from the bottom. On the other end, cut a slit half way down from the top. Be careful not to cut all the way through.

3. Bend or fold (each will give a different look) the strip and fit one slit into the other.

4. Toss your fish in the air and watch it twirl!

Air Fun

God give us some gifts we cannot even see. One of these gifts is air. We could not live more than a few minutes without the air that we breathe. Air is partly made of oxygen. Plants give off oxygen so that there is always plenty for us to breathe. God planned it that way.

A Flyer

1. Fold a sheet of paper in half. Open.

2. Fold the two upper corners toward the center.

3. Turn it over and fold an upper corner to the center line.

4. Fold again (same side, same direction) to the center line.

5. Do the same with the other side.

6. Turn it over and fold the outer edges to the center.

7. Hold the flyer by the original fold underneath and send it off.

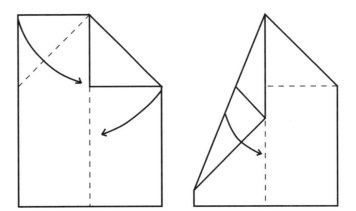

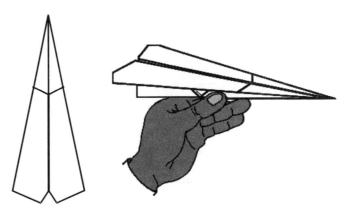

Blow Out

1. Fold a sheet of paper into thirds and cut off one strip.

2. Color one side of this strip.

3. Roll the strip into a tube. Tape the length of the tube and one end.

4. Roll up the tube starting from the taped end. Use those good lungs God gave you to blow out your blow out.

43

Parachute

1. Fold and cut a sheet of paper into fourths.

2. Fold each fourth in half lengthwise and cut. You now have eight strips of paper. Each strip will be a parachute.

3. Fold each strip in half, open, and draw a line down the center from one end of the strip to the fold. Cut along this line. Turn these two wings different directions. On the plain end, draw a person.

4. Add a paper clip to the bottom for weight. Toss your parachute up high and watch it whirl down.

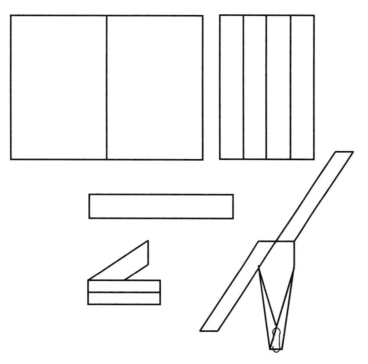

Helicopter

The helicopter is made the same as the parachute, starting with smaller pieces of paper.

1. Fold and cut a sheet of paper in half.

2. Fold a half in half and cut it. Fold each of these halves in half and cut so that you have four strips.

3. Complete steps 3 and 4 of "Parachute," except for drawing a person. Fold the edges of the bottom in just a little before you add the paper clip.

Windmill

1. Start with a square of any size. Color both sides.

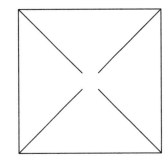

2. Fold the square into a triangle, open and fold into a triangle again from the other direction. Open. Cut along each crease almost to the center.

3. Bend the four corners into the center and staple or tape.

4. Roll a half-inch wide strip of paper into a small cylinder. Tape or glue.

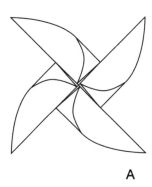

A

5. Roll a sheet of paper into a cylinder and tape or glue.

6. Straighten a paper clip (or use a more pliable craft wire) to run through A, B, and C. Flatten this wire at the front of the windmill and at the back of the cylinder. Tape the wire to the cylinder.

   (To make your windmill more sturdy, use a length of wire doubled. Before inserting the two wires through A, B, and C, wrap a tiny strip of paper, or string around the bend in the wire, to create a ball on the end of the wire that will keep the windmill from slipping off. Then this double wire can be inserted through the pieces, folded open (and taped) in opposite directions on the cylinder.)

C

B

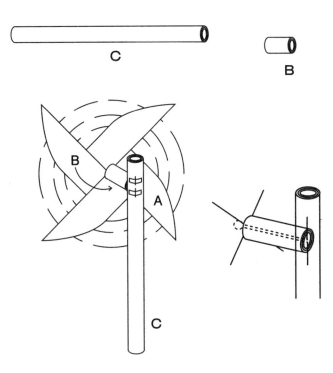

B

A

C

7. Use your lung power or the wind to set your windmill spinning, or run, or twirl around.

Your Own Art Show

Quick-Change Art:
A Pig to a Cat

1. Cut 3 1/2 inches off the side of a sheet of paper so that you are left with a piece that is 5 inches wide and 11 inches long.

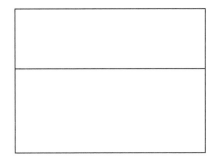

2. Fold another sheet of paper in half, and reopen. On one side of this sheet, cut four slits 1/4-inch from the fold to within 1/4-inch of the edge. Make the first slit 1 1/2 inches from the top of the page, the second slit 1 1/2 inches below the first slit, and so on.

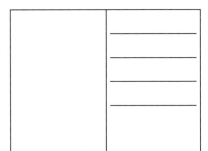

3. Thread the long thin paper through the slits and refold the other half of the larger paper behind the threaded paper.

4. Using the sample as a guide, draw a cat.

5. Move the center paper up or down until you have blank paper between parts of the cat, and draw the rest of the pig, using the parts that already show.

6. Now you can move your center paper up and down and watch the cat change into a pig and the pig change into a cat!

In real life, do cats change into pigs, or anything other than cats? No, because when God created the world, He said that each animal would "produce more of its own kind." This means that pigs will always give birth to pigs, cats will give birth to cats, and people will give birth to people. Think what a mess we'd have if this were not true!

Quick-Change Art:
A Happy Boy to a Sad Man

1. Fold and cut a sheet of paper in half.

2. Fold a half in half. Draw half an oval shape with an ear in the center.

3. Open the paper and finish the face. Draw two eyes on the same level as the ears. Draw hair at the top and make a reddish brown curve in the center. Draw a squiggly line mouth but don't color it. (Pattern on page 93.)

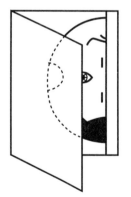

4. Turn the paper upside down and the face should look like a sad man with a beard and a bald head. Cut out the head, allowing some hair to extend past the oval.

5. Fold the other sheet of paper in half for a cover.

6. Glue or tape the head to the inside of the cover with the face across the fold. Glue the ears only. The face should fold out for a three-dimensional effect when the card is opened.

7. You and a friend can take turns trying to guess if you will open the card to see the happy boy or the sad man.

When we ask the Lord Jesus to forgive our sins, He does. He helps us make the right decisions while we are living here on earth, and will take us to live with Him in Heaven some day. Knowing this gives us joy that no amount of trouble can take away. Then our faces look like the happy face. But sometimes we do wrong things. We may stop talking to God in prayer. We may forget to read the Bible to find out what God wants us to do. We may lose the joyful feeling we once had and become sad. Then we look like the sad face. But when we ask God to forgive us and tell Him that we still love Him, God brings the joyous sunshine back into our lives, and we look like the happy face again.

Create a Picture
Out of the Black

1. Using felt-tip pens or water-color markers, cover a sheet of paper with brilliant patches color—no pictures yet, just color.

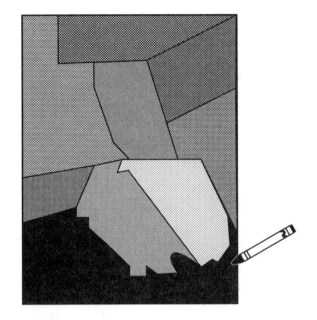

2. Cover the entire page with black crayon.

3. Using an object like a coin, nail file, key, or fingernail (messy!), scratch a picture through the black crayon so that your colors show through.

4. You may use this picture for the outside of a greeting card by coloring only the bottom half of a page and folding the top half down behind it.

Sometimes our lives seem plain and boring. Sometimes we look at the people on television and in the magazines and we think that we are not pretty or handsome enough.

But God tells us in His Word that He does not judge our beauty by what we look like on the outside, but by what we look like on the inside. Does this mean that God judges us by our veins and bones and muscles? No, it means that he judges us by our thoughts and actions.

When we are kind to others, when we share happily, when we are eager to help our parents, God looks at us and thinks we are beautiful! And, because this is God's world, when He finds beauty in our lives, others see it too! In this way, God can make a "pretty picture" out of every person's life.

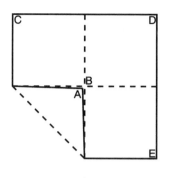

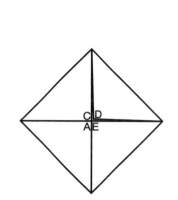

Frame a Picture

1. Start with a square. Fold it in half from both directions to find the center.

2. Open the square and fold each corner to meet in the center.

3. Take each point in the center and fold it back to the edge.

4. Color or paste a picture in the center square, or insert a photo, or print your favorite Bible verse.

5. Decorate the frame, if you like.

6. Create a sturdy rest for your frame by folding a sheet of paper into fourths, lengthwise. Fold this strip in half, and tape each end to the back of your frame.

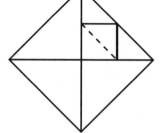

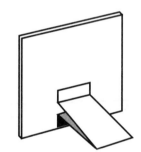

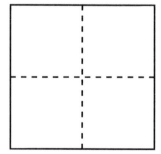

Abstract Art

1. Start with a square.

2. Color one side brilliantly in various shades.

3. Fold the square into fourths. Then fold point to point so you have a triangle with eight layers.

4. Cut designs into the triangle.

5. Open the paper and glue it to a plain square. Tape string to the back to hang it up, or fold it in half (with the blank paper on the inside) for a pretty card. Write your message inside.

A Paper Zoo

"So God created the large sea animals. He created every living thing that moves in the sea. The sea is filled with these living things. Each one produces more of its own kind. God also made every bird that flies. And each bird produces more if its own kind.

"Then God said, 'Let the earth be filled with animals. And let each produce more of its own kind. Let there be tame animals and small crawling animals and wild animals. And let each produce more of its kind.' And it happened."

—Genesis 1:21, 25

Snake

When Satan persuaded the lady Eve to disobey God, he appeared to her in the form of a snake. Let's make a wiggly snake.

1. Fold a sheet of paper until you have eight sections.

2. Color all the strips on both sides, then cut them apart. (Save one to make the caterpillar on page 52.)

3. Tape the seven strips together, end to end.

4. Carefully cut this long narrow strip into two thinner strips. (Or, to make a bigger snake, tape two rows of four strips together, using the entire sheet of paper.)

5. Tape two of your strips together at right angles.

6. Fold A over B and B over A. Continue doing this, always folding the paper on top of the last fold.

7. When you use up all the paper, cut out a paper head an attach it to the end of the snake. Add a tiny red paper tongue.

Satan tries to get us to disobey God, but if God's Spirit is living inside of us, He will help us say "No!" to Satan!

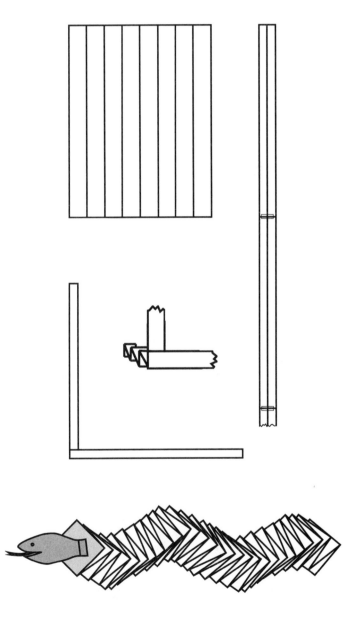

Caterpillar

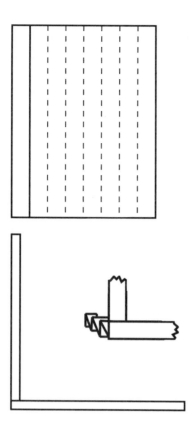

1. Fold a sheet of paper lengthwise until you have eight sections.

2. Cut off one section. Color it brown or gray on both sides.

3. Fold and cut in half lengthwise into two long strips.

4. Tape or glue these strips at right angles.

5. Fold strip A over strip B. Fold strip B back over strip A. Continue folding back and forth until strips are used up.

6. Glue the ends together and draw the face. Add tiny paper antenna.

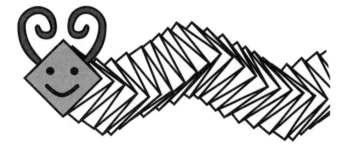

A caterpillar is a fuzzy little creature that crawls on the ground. But God has a big surprise for this wee fellow. One day he will prepare a snug little bed for himself and go to sleep for a long time. When he awakens, a wonderful change has occurred; he has turned into a beautiful butterfly! He can then spread his wings and fly away to a new life!

God also has a new life in store for us. When we die, God will give us a new body and all the freedom and joy of everlasting life in Heaven. But, we will receive these wonderful gifts only if we have loved God and accepted His Son Jesus as our Savior.

Now let's look at the next page and make two beautiful butterflies.

Butterfly One

1. Cut a sheet of paper into fourths.

2. Color sections A and B on both sides.

3. Pleat section A, folding from the long side.

4. Pleat section B from the short side.

5. Fold section C into four stripes. Cut off one strip.

6. Color the strip brown or black. Roll it into a tight cylinder. Tape or glue it.

7. Fold the cylinder in half and streak with glue. Assemble butterfly.

8. When glue has dried, slit the upper end into two antenna.

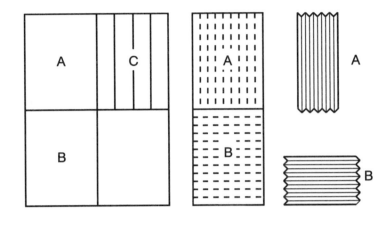

1/4 of C

Butterfly Two

1. Fold and cut a sheet of paper in half. Color one piece on both sides. (Or, colored magazine pages work very well for this caper.)

2. Fold it in half lengthwise. Using the pattern from page 94, cut a shape like this along the fold.

3. Beginning at the bottom, fold pleats as narrow as possible.

4. Wrap three inches of chenille wire (or a twist tie) around the center for the butterfly's body and antennae.

These butterflies can be used to decorate gift packages, or you might make a mobile with them! Can you think of some more uses for pretty "flutterbys"?

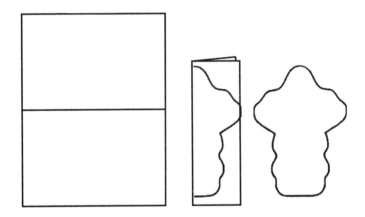

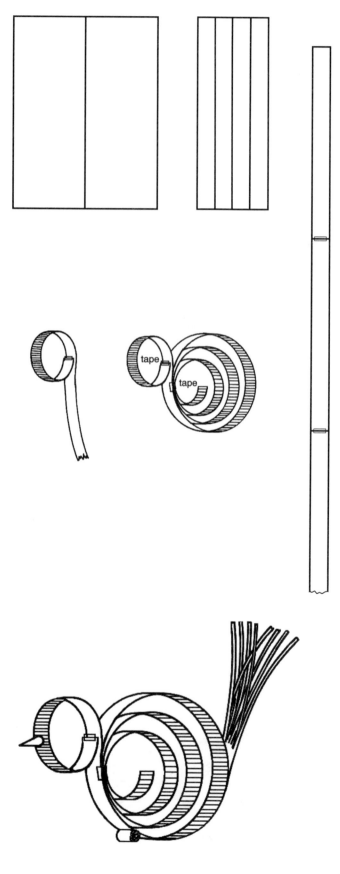

Bird of Paradise

1. Fold and cut a sheet of paper in half.

2. Color both sides of one of the halves.

3. Fold the sheet into four strips and cut them apart.

4. Tape three of the strips end to end.

5. Form a circle for the head about two inches across, and tape it.

6. For the body of the bird, roll end A around a pencil until you reach the head. Remove the pencil and tape the body to the head.

7. To form the tail, cut the remaining strip in half and cut one of these strips into the narrowest strips you can, leaving at least 1/4 inch uncut at the end. Tape this end to the body.

8. To form the beak, cut 1/2 inch from the remaining strip and roll into a cone shape. Trim the wide end until it is flat. Dip this flat end into some glue and hold it against the bird's head until it sticks.

9. The bird is top heavy and wants to fall forward. To stop this, roll the remaining strip of paper into a cylinder and glue it to the bottom of the bird at the point where you want the forward roll to stop.

(For more birds, see pages 82 and 83.)

A Flying Bird

1. Fold and cut a sheet of paper in half.

2. Fold a half in half and draw a bird on it. (Pattern on page 87.)

3. Color and cut out the bird on the double piece of paper so you have two birds.

4. Glue the body and head together with the end of a two-foot length of string between them. Do not glue the wings or tail feathers.

5. Roll up the other half of the paper and tie the end of the string to this roll. Spread the bird's wings. Hold the roll of paper and run with your bird fluttering behind you.

Any Animal You Want

1. Fold and cut a sheet of paper in half.

2. Fold each section in half. (Obviously, larger animals may be made using larger pieces of paper.)

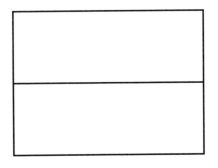

3. Draw, color, and cut animals from this double paper.

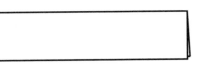

4. Glue the two animal pieces together except for the ears and legs, which will open so that your animal can stand. Spread its ears apart.

5. Color your animals.

Dragon's Head

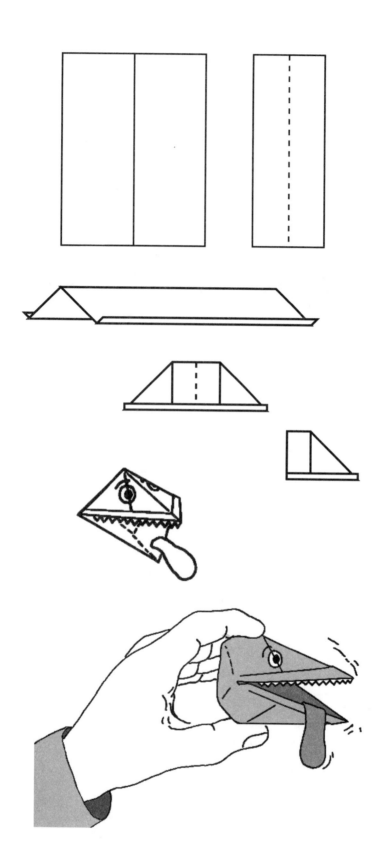

1. Fold and cut a sheet of paper in half.

2. Color one of the halves on both sides. One side is the outside of the dragon's head. The other side is the inside of the mouth.

3. Fold the paper in half lengthwise. Fold up each side about one-quarter inch.

4. Fold each end into a triangle and tuck the bottom of each triangle inside the quarter-inch fold.

5. Fold this shape in half, crease, and open it. Place both thumbs inside the crease you have just made and carefully pull the sides all the way out until the top and bottom points come together.

6. Tape a row of teeth inside the mouth. Glue a long red tongue to the throat. Color two big eyes.

7. You can use this dragon as a talking puppet by placing your thumb on the bottom point and your fingers on the top, or you can crease the back of its head to get the mouth to stay closed.

Mr. Big Mouth

1. Start with a square.

2. Fold the square in half, open it, turn the paper and fold it in half again from the other direction. Open it up again. (This is simply to find the center of the paper.)

3. Fold each of the four corners into the center.

4. Turn your paper over and make a smaller square by folding each of the four corners into the center again.

5. Glue these four triangles down and color this side of the paper red because it will be the inside of the big mouth. (You may use a magic marker because there are enough layers of paper to keep the red from bleeding through to the outside layer.)

6. Turn the paper over and fold it once more into a triangle. Draw two eyes and nose holes and color the rest of Mr. Big Mouth as you wish. You may also cut out a tongue and glue it inside the mouth.

7. Slip your thumb into the square on the bottom and your first two fingers in the into the square on top.and discover how to make Mr. Big Mouth talk.

8. To keep your fingers from slipping out as Mr. Big Mouth talks, roll two small strips of paper into cylinders and glue them inside the squares where you place your fingers.

9. Now Mr. Big Mouth is ready to talk to you and to help you say a great big "Thank You, God, for giving me a mouth and a voice that I can use to praise You!"

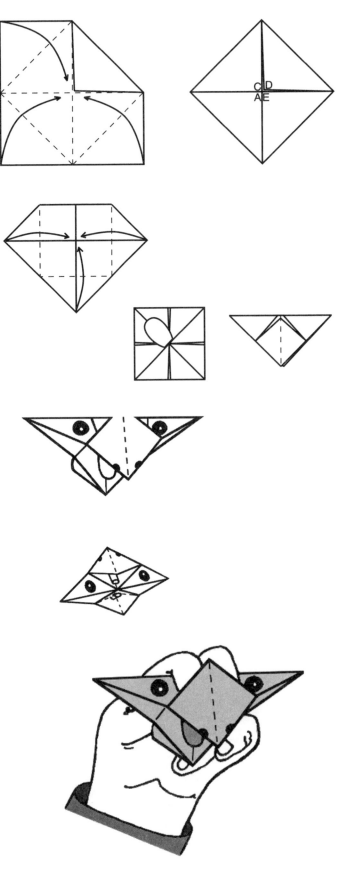

Toys That Move

Toys cannot do anything or go anywhere without your help. Neither would we be able to live or move without the gift of life that God has given us. When we let Him, God is happy to guide us and help us.

A Doll With Movable Head and Legs

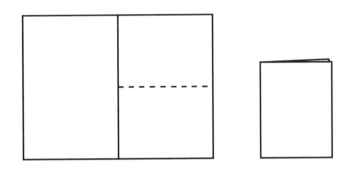

1. Fold and cut a sheet of paper in half.

2. Fold one half in half.

3. Draw a body without legs or a head in shorts or a dress. (The bigger the clothes, the better.) Cut the body out of both sheets.

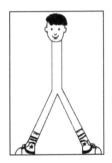

4. Color one of the bodies as the front and color the other one as the back.

5. Take the other 1/2 piece of paper. On this sheet, draw a very thin body with a head, to fit inside the clothes you have drawn.

6. Glue the front and the back of the clothing pieces together around the body. Be very careful to put glue only on the very edges of your paper. Have fun wiggling the legs and head!

Patterns on page 95.

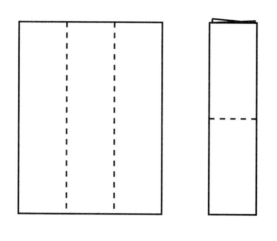

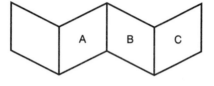

A Pocket Puppet

1. Fold a sheet of paper in thirds, lengthwise. Fold the thirds in half.

2. Fold the outer two edges back again so that the paper looks like a "W."

3. Close the paper and you will have four squares in layers. Color A and B squares to look like the inside of a mouth. Color C with eyes and a nose. You may add a beak, if you like. Give the mouth a tongue and a row of teeth.

4. Glue the top layer to the second layer and the bottom layer to the third layer.

5. To move your puppet, slip your fingers in the pocket behind the eyes and your thumb in the bottom pocket. Now you can make your puppet speak!

A Flip Book

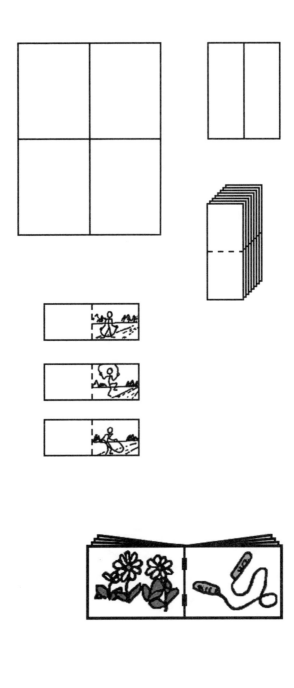

1. Fold and cut a sheet of paper into fourths.

2. Fold and cut each piece in half lengthwise.

3. Line up these eight strips of paper. Fold the group in half and fasten the pages of your book together the best way you can. The easiest way is to put a staple or two right in the middle of the book. Or, you can glue each fold onto the fold of the pages that come before it, but you must be careful not to get glue all over your pages. Or, you can use a tiny strip of tape to tape each page to the one before it. When you finish, the middle pages of the book will be sticking out further than the outside pages. Trim these carefully to make the edge of your book as even as possible.

4. Decorate the cover of your book.

5. Inside, on each right-hand page, draw one or two stick figures in different positions. Try to make each drawing just a little bit different from the one just before it. Then, as you flip through the book, the characters will look as though they are moving!

Instead of figures, you might show flowers and a tree growing up out of the ground. On each page the tree gets just a little bit taller and more flowers spring up. Or perhaps you could show a bunch of balloons drifting up from the bottom left to the top right of your page.

Experiment with this paper caper until you get something that looks like a motion picture. Do you know what you have just created? A cartoon! This is exactly how cartoonists create TV shows and movies—every single movement is created by many different drawings. Each drawing becomes a frame of film that is quickly "flipped" by your eyes!

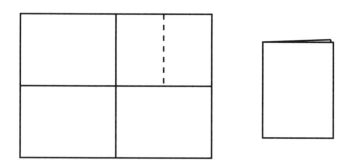

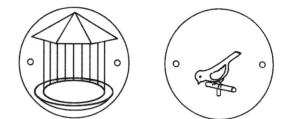

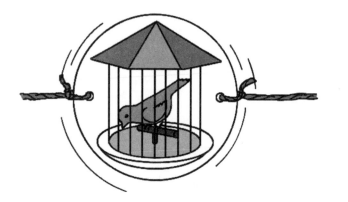

Twirl a Moving Picture

1. Fold and cut a sheet of paper into fourths.

2. Fold a small piece of paper in half and glue together to make it thicker. Trace a circle as large as possible. Cut it out.

3. Draw a bird on one side and a cage on the other side.

4. Poke two small holes near the edges of the circle. Put about eight inches of thread through the holes.

5. Hold the ends of the thread in your hands and blow on the circle. Look quickly and you will see the bird inside the cage.

6. Try different pictures like a pig in a pen, or a picture on a TV screen.

A Walking Doll

1. Fold and cut a sheet of paper in half.

2. Fold one piece in half and sketch a doll without legs on it. (Try to use more of the area available than is shown in the sketch. The bigger your doll is, the easier it will be to fit your fingers through the slit.)

3. Cut out your two identical dolls.

4. Color one of the dolls as the front, color the other doll as the back. Cut a slit across the back doll.

5. Glue both dolls together but put no glue beneath the slit.

6. Place two of your fingers through the slit and walk your doll using your fingers as the legs.

   To make this doll more sturdy, cut the doll out of four layers and glue the two backs and two fronts together, or try using a heavier kind of paper.

A Surprise Book

1. Fold and cut a sheet of paper in half.

2. Place one half on top of the other and fold into a book.

3. Glue, tape or staple your pages together. On each page, lightly draw two fine lines about 1 3/4 inches from the top and from the bottom, to divide each page into thirds.

4. Draw and color a different person or creature on each page. Try to keep the head in the top section, the torso in the middle and the legs in the bottom. Also try to keep the width of each figure about the same where they will meet on the various pages.

5. Close the book. On the top three pages, cut along your penciled lines from the outside edge almost to the center, making three equal sections. Erase the lines on the fourth page.

6. See what funny combinations you can make by moving the flaps.

Aren't you glad that people and animals aren't all mixed up like the funny combinations you have made? If creatures changed from what God created, we might have ended up with a mess! But God created people, animals, birds, fish, insects and reptiles so that each reproduces more of its own kind. This is God's world and He planned it that way.

The Juggler

1. Start with two full pieces of paper. Roll and tape one into a cylinder lengthwise. Wrap the other paper widthwise around this long cylinder and tape it to fit snugly.

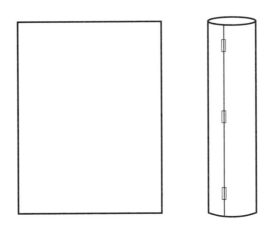

2. On the outside cylinder, draw a juggler—a stick figure is good enough. (Hint: If the juggler is too wide and the corresponding holes are spread out too much, the final movement of the balls is difficult to see.)

3. Remove the inside cylinder. On the outside cylinder, punch holes above and around the juggler. Use a paper punch, scissors, pencil, or any sharp tool.

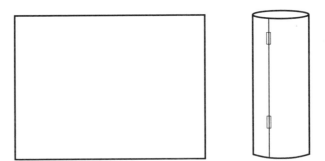

4. Tape two strips of scrap paper across the top of the outside cylinder. These will keep the inside cylinder from extending past the top when it is being turned. Replace the inside cylinder and align the two taped edges.

5. Being careful not to get any color on the outside cylinder, color a bright ball inside the first hole. Turn the inside cylinder just until the first ball disappears and color a second ball through the second hole. Turn again and color the third ball through the third hole. Continue in this way until you get all around the juggler. These balls should all be the same color. (If you do get color on the outside cylinder, remove the inside and paint around the edges of your holes with correction fluid or any other thick white paint.)

6. If you wish, you may start a second and a third ball, each of a different color, following the first. Leave at least one empty space between the two balls.

7. By turning the inside paper around, the colored balls appear to be in motion.

Baskets

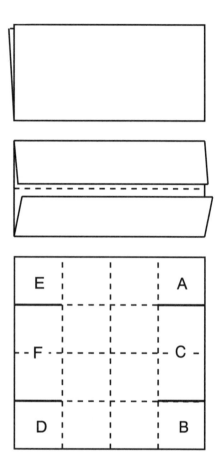

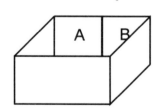

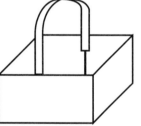

A Large Basket

1. Start with a square (save the scrap). Color the square on both sides.

2. Fold in half, open. Fold the top down to the center crease. Fold the bottom up to the center crease, making four sections.

3. Open and fold the same way in the other direction, for a total of sixteen squares.

4. Cut along the four lines indicated.

5. Form into a basket using the center four squares as a base. Glue or tape A and B inside C, and D and E inside F.

6. Cut a handle from the strip you cut off to make the square. Color it and tape it to the opposite sides of your basket.

A Small Basket

Once a boy went to hear Jesus teach. The boy brought with him a picnic lunch in a basket—five bread buns and two fish. Do you know what happened to that boy's lunch? Turn to John 6 to find out.

1. Using a square made from 1/2 piece of paper, form a small basket the same way you made the big one.

2. From one of the leftover pieces of paper, cut out five loaves and two fishes.

A Tulip Basket

1. Start with a square (save the scrap). Fold the square into fourths, then fold again into a triangle.

2. Draw and cut out this shape. The more you leave uncut at A and B, the bigger the base of your basket will be.

3. Open the paper which should look something like a wheel. Color it.

4. Form the basket by folding up and taping (on the inside) A over B, B over C, C over D and so on around the circle.

5. Cut, color and fasten a handle from the strip you cut off to make the square.

Now that you know how, you can make baskets of many different sizes for many different uses. Use heavy paper (like a grocery bag) to make a basket that is strong enough to carry things. Use pretty wrapping paper to make a basket to hold a surprise gift for a friend. Make several small baskets to fill with candy for a birthday party. What else could you do with your paper baskets?

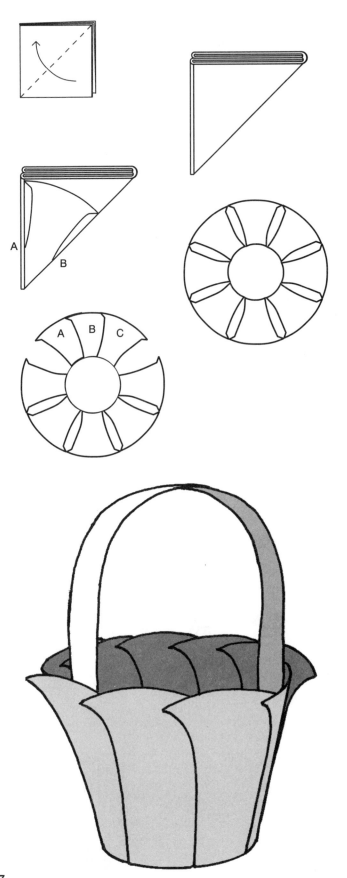

Dress Like a Queen or a King

A beautiful queen from Arabia heard that King Solomon of Palestine was the smartest person in the world. She visited him to find out if this was true, and asked him many hard questions. She discovered that he was not only very smart, he was also very rich. When the queen visited King Solomon, she wore her finest clothes and jewelry. Let us make jewelry and pretend we are the queen or the king.

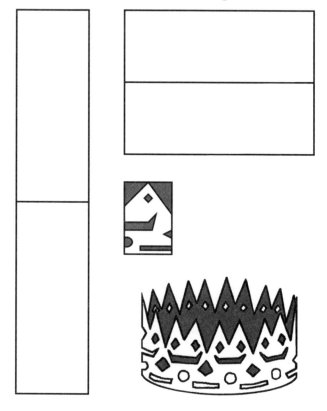

A Crown

1. Fold and cut a sheet of paper in half lengthwise.

2. Tape the pieces end to end and.color them on one side.

3. Fit the paper around your head and tape it where it feels best.

4. Fold the crown in half three times. Cut and snip with scissors.

5. Unfold your crown. You may decorate it with scraps of colored paper, or thread yarn through the holes, or add glitter and sequins.

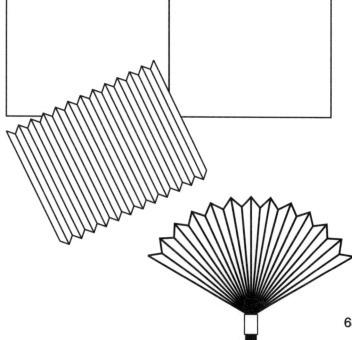

A Royal Fan

1. Tape or glue two full sheets of paper together end to end. Color both sides.

2. Beginning at one end, pleat the paper all the way to the other end.

3. Tape the bottom of the fan tightly. Use the fan to cool yourself on a hot day.

68

A Quick Necklace

1. Color a piece of paper brilliantly on both sides. (Or use gift wrap paper, etc.)

2. Fold and cut the paper in half length-wise.

3. Cut each half into narrow strips.

4. Tape strips into interlocking rings until your necklace is as long as you want it.

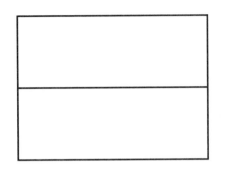

A Link Bracelet

1. Color a piece of paper on one side.

2. Fold and cut the paper into fourths.

3. Fold and cut each fourth in half length-wise.

4. Fold one of these small pieces in half, then fold in half again in the same direction so you have four thicknesses.

5. Fold in half again and cut this shape along the fold. (Or trace the full-size pattern on the four thicknesses.)

6. Open the paper and you should have four bracelet links this shape.

7. Cut four links from each of the other small pieces of paper.

8. Fold each link in half and slip through the top of another link to form a bracelet.

9. Tape the last link to the first after it is on your wrist, or make the bracelet big enough to slip on and off.

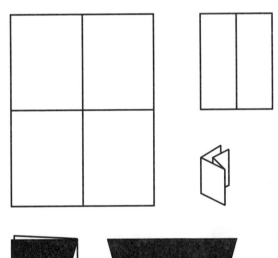

FULL SIZE

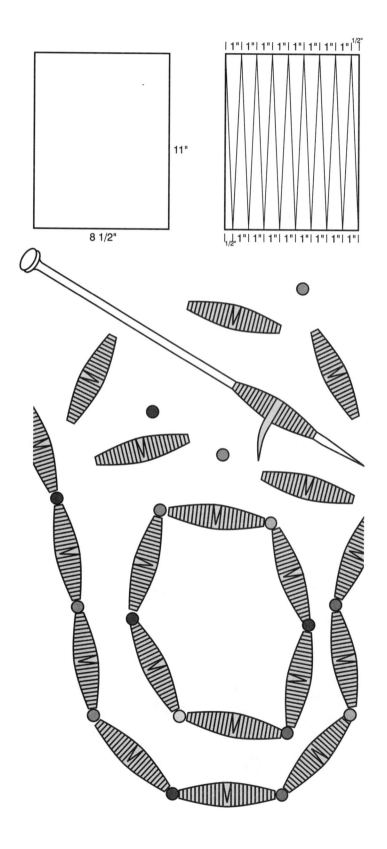

A Longer-Lasting Necklace

1. Color a sheet of paper brilliantly on one side (or use colored magazine pages or wallpaper).

2. Rule and cut into long triangles an inch wide at the broadest part. Throw away the 1/2" strips at each end.

3. Find a round object such as a knitting needle or a nail. Roll a long strip of paper around the nail, beginning at the wide end. When you reach about two inches from the pointed end, squeeze a thin line of white glue and roll to the point.

4. You should have a pretty oval-shaped bead. Slide it off the round object and let the glue dry. One sheet of paper forms sixteen one-inch beads, so you will need another sheet for a string long enough to go over your head.

5. String the beads on any cord that is handy and tie the ends. Elastic cord is nice, especially for a bracelet. If you have any small round beads, string one between each paper bead.

6. These beads are prettier and last longer if coated with colorless nail polish or sprayed with clear gloss. Coating each bead with glue as you make it will also provide a long-lasting, glossy finish.

7. Now make a matching bracelet!

A Belt or Hair Band

1. Fold and cut a sheet of paper into fourths.

2. Fold a fourth in half lengthwise and open.

3. Fold each edge to meet at the crease in the center.

4. Fold again so you have a long, narrow strip of four thicknesses. Color one side.

5. Fold in half and then fold again so the two ends meet in the center. This is a belt link.

6. Do this with the other three pieces you cut. You may need six or more sheets of paper to have enough links for a belt.

7. Fasten the links together by placing one link through the loops of another link. If you always hold the links so that the folded edges are on top, the links will slide together without catching inside a fold. Your belt should look something like this.

8. Add more links until the belt fits around your waist. Fasten a cord to the link on each end and tie around your waist.

9. For the headband, fit the chain to your head, then fasten the last link to the first. The headband will stretch enough to put on, yet will fit snugly.

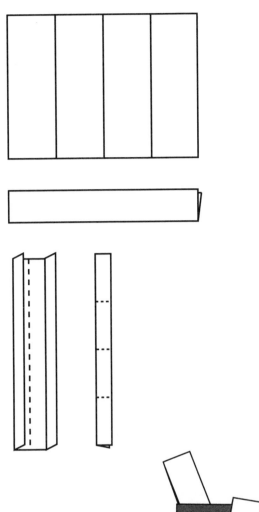

Greeting Cards

Many of the paper capers in this book can be used as covers for greeting cards. When you think of a special message you would like to send to someone, look for a paper caper to use as a card. Make up your own messages to fit with your own art. Here are some very special pop-up card ideas.

"Meet My Friend" Card

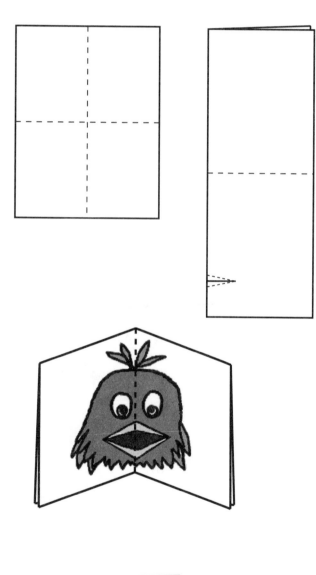

1. Fold a sheet of paper into fourths. Open it lengthwise only. On the lower half, cut a 1 1/4-inch slash 1 1/2 inch from the bottom.

2. Fold upwards and downwards around the slash.

3. Open the paper and see what can be made into a large mouth. Fold the upper half of the paper down behind the mouth. (This will be the cover of the card.) Partly close the card and pull the lips of the mouth toward you, so they will open and close as the card does.

4. Color an animal's head around the mouth, giving it big eyes. Color the inside of the mouth red. Add a tongue and teeth if you like.

5. Decorate the front of the card with a picture and the message, "Meet My Friend," or make up a funny message of your own.

The front cover can be glued to the inside if you like, but be careful not to get any glue on the lips. Gluing the cover to the inside is not necessary.

"I Like You" Card

1. Fold and cut a sheet of paper in half.

2. Fold one piece in half and make a triangular fold about two inches from the top. Open the paper and push the fold inside.

3. Open and close the card and you will find that the inverted triangle pops up. Draw and color something that uses this pop-up idea.

4. The sample shows the triangle colored like a basket, with flowers and leaves drawn on scrap paper and glued to the basket. You may think of another way to use the pop-up triangle. (Be sure that your flowers, or whatever you put here, do not extend beyond the edge of the card when it is closed.)

5. Glue a cover sheet to the card. Avoid putting glue on the pop-up triangle. Decorate the cover. The sample says, "I will surprise you because I like you."

A Secret Code

You can send a card to a friend that contains a message written in a secret code. Use this paper caper to help you.

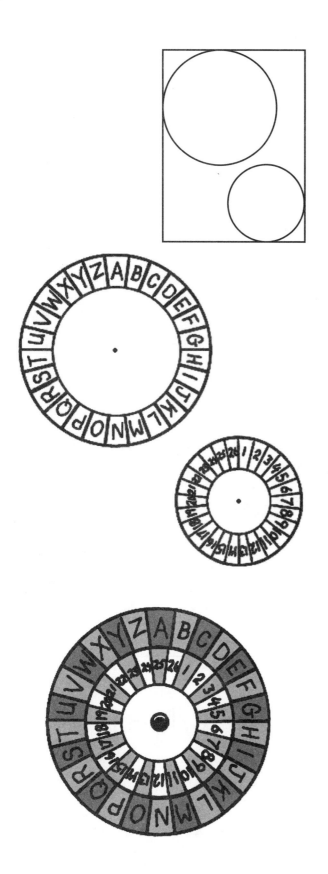

1. From a sheet of paper trace two circles one larger than the other.

2. Fasten the smaller circle on top of the larger circle with a paper fastener in the center. (It will be easier to do steps three and four if you simply tape the two circles in place first. Draw the lines all the way across both circles, then insert the paper fastener.)

3. Divide the outside space into twenty-six areas and print one letter of the alphabet in each.

4. Divide the inside space into twenty-six areas and write the numbers, one to twenty-six.

5. Place the two circles so, for example, five is beside G. Tell your friend the code is 5-G when you send your message.

6. Now, see if you can decode this message from God to you (written in 5-G):

7 10 13 20 3 23 13 19

Decorations

We know that God enjoys beauty because He created such a beautiful world. God's Word also tells us that He has prepared a beautiful place in Heaven for every person who accepts the Lord Jesus as his or her Savior.

We can make some beautiful things to enjoy right now. As you make these things, thank God for the beauty He has created.

A Flower

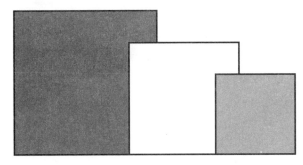

1. Use as many sheets of paper as you like to give you squares of various sizes. An 8 1/2-inch square, 6 1/2-inch square, and 4 1/2-inch square work well. Use smaller squares to end up with smaller flowers. (But they are harder to cut.)

2. Color each square differently.

3. Fold each square in half, point to point to form a triangle.

4. Fold again into a smaller triangle, then fold into thirds.

5. With strong scissors, round off the top of the flower petal. The sharper the curve, the more separated your petals will be.

6. Make snips in both sides of your petals. You can snip the top rounded edge too, but then the finished product looks more like a snowflake than a flower.

7. Glue or staple the petals together, working from largest to smallest.

If your scissors are not sharp enough, cut your flower from the small triangle (step 4-A). The flower will then have four petals instead of six.

A Lacy Festoon

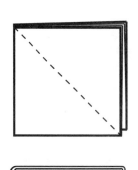

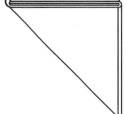

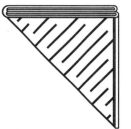

1. Start with a square.

2. Brilliantly color both sides or leave it white.

3. Fold twice to get a smaller square. Fold point to point so you have a triangle eight layers thick.

4. Cut narrow slits from alternate sides not quite to the edges of the triangle.

5. Open it carefully and hang the festoon wherever it looks best.

A Six-Point Snowflake

1. Start with a square.

2. Fold the square into a triangle. Fold again to find the center. Open last fold.

3. From the center of the triangle, fold point A at an angle past side C.

4. Fold point B at an angle past side D. You may have to refold in order to make the sides align as in the diagram.

5. Fold in half. Cut a scalloped border on the side of the layer folds. Make fancy snips along the solid fold.

6. Open the snowflake. You can glue it to a square you have colored brilliantly. Or attach several by threads to the ceiling and watch them sway in a gentle breeze.

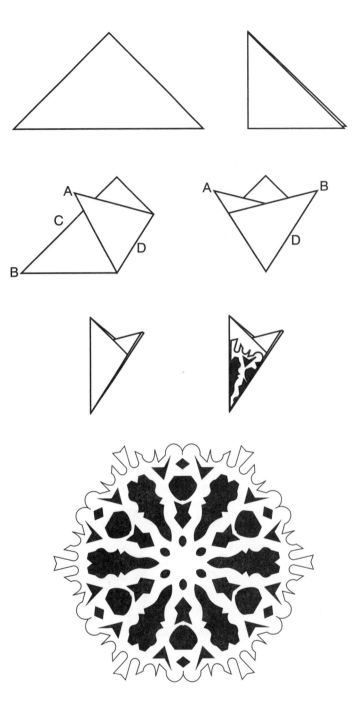

A Swing Thing

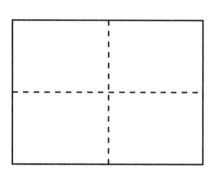

1. Fold and cut a sheet of paper into fourths.

2. Color each section a different shade, on one side.

3. Fold each small section into fourths.

4. From these four layers, cut out the shape shown. The top of the triangle must be at the single fold in the paper. (When you cut this shape out, the double folds on the side will be cut off.)

5. Fit the shapes together by sliding the links through the open space at the top of each triangle.

6. You will have a string of eight links from one sheet of paper. Make your chain as long and colorful as you wish. Hang it by a thread at the top for an ornament or room decoration, or make yourself a belt or necklace.

Pattern is on page 96.

A Book Cover

1. To make a cover for your favorite book, you must first measure the book. Open the book, holding the pages up so that the front and back covers lie flat on the table. Measure the distance from the edge of one cover to the far edge of the other, and from the top of the book to the bottom.

2. Add two inches to the height and two inches to the width. This is the size of paper you must begin with to make your cover.

3. Fold this sheet of paper in half. Open it and center the backbone of the book over this center, folded line. Mark the width of the backbone on the paper.

4. Fold the paper in half again and cut one-inch squares from the outside corners. On the inside corners (the ones next to the fold), cut out the paper between the marks you made when measuring the backbone. Cut one-inch deep, no matter how wide.

5. Open the sheet and fold in the one inch border between the dotted lines. Fold the top sections down, the bottom ones up, and the side flaps inward.

6. Decorate this cover and fold it around your book. The inside corners may be taped for added security.

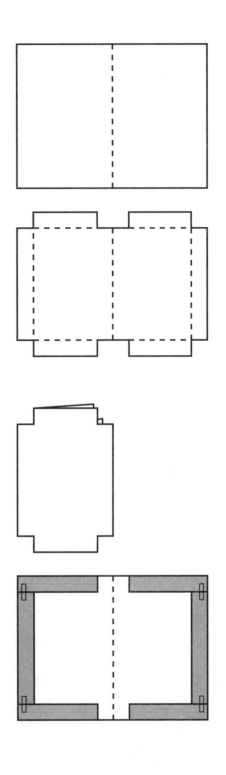

81

Mobiles

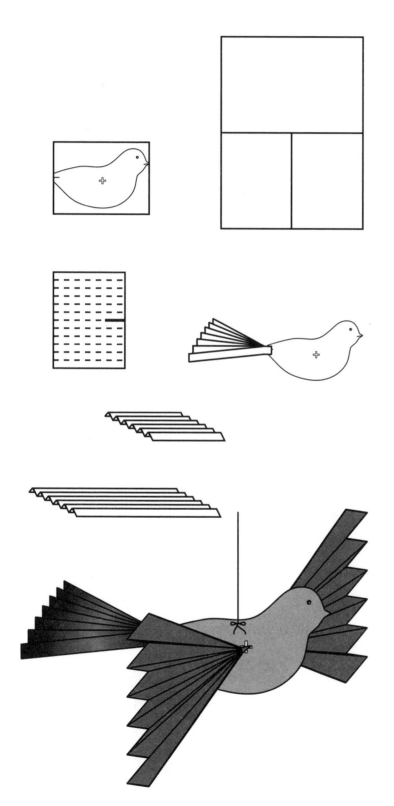

Fancy Birds

1. Fold and cut a sheet of paper into three parts as shown.

2. On one of the smaller pieces, draw a bird without wings or a tail. Cut it out and color both sides.

   (Pattern is on page 96.)

3. For the bird's tail, color the other small piece in a different shade and pleat it. In the center of one side cut a slit about an inch long. (See the heavy line.)

4. Place the rear of the bird in the slit and tape the pleats to both sides of the bird.

5. Cut a 1/2-inch slit (either horizontal or vertical) in the side of the bird.

6. For the bird's wings, color and pleat the large piece of paper.

7. Before opening up the pleat, draw it half way through the slit in the bird so there is a wing on each side. (The wings can be inserted either horizontally or vertically.) Place tape around the hole to keep it from tearing.

8. Tape a thread to the bird's back, hang him up, and watch him fly. Make several different colored birds for your mobile.

Have you ever thought how a young robin must feel when making his first flight to the warm southland in autumn? He has never been away from his own neighborhood and he must wonder why he is leaving it, and where he is going. When God created birds like the robin, whose food of worms and insects is not available in cold weather, He created in them the instinct that causes them to fly south where they have plenty of food to eat. God planned it that way.

Small Birds

1. Start with a square.

2. Fold and cut into fourths.

3. Fold each small square point to point into a triangle.

4. Fold each point up, about half an inch from the center fold.

5. Turn the bird over so the center fold is on the bottom. Color the front peak like a head. Color the wings and tail. Make short scissor snips to fringe them.

6. Run a triangle of thread from the supporting pole to the bird, along an inch and a half or two inches of the bird's body, and back up to the pole. This triangular-shaped thread will keep your birds from doing a nose-dive toward the floor.

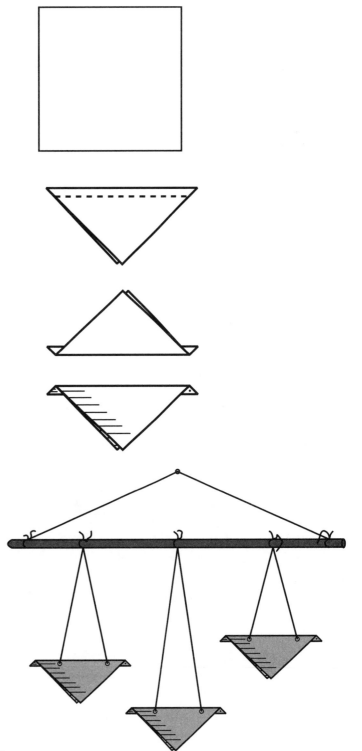

83

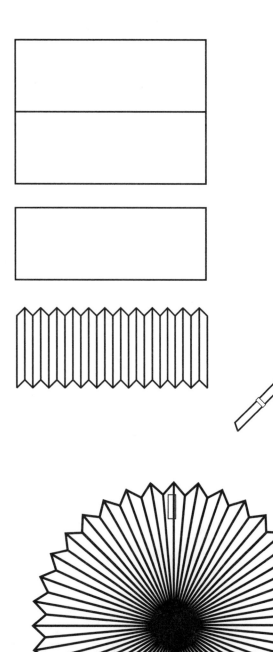

Medallions or Flowers

1. Fold and cut a sheet of paper in half lengthwise.

2. Beginning at one end of a long piece, pleat the paper to the other end.

3. Open the paper and color every other section a different shade, or decorate any way you like.

4. Refold, and cut each end on an angle.

5. Place a narrow tape tightly around the center. Draw folds together in a circle and tape both sides. Hang it up, wear it on a cord around your neck, or slip a bobby pin under the tape and wear it in your hair.

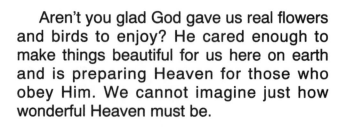

Aren't you glad God gave us real flowers and birds to enjoy? He cared enough to make things beautiful for us here on earth and is preparing Heaven for those who obey Him. We cannot imagine just how wonderful Heaven must be.

Floating Flowers

1. Start with a square.

2. Fold the square in half. Open. Fold the top down to the center crease. Fold the bottom up to the center crease. Open. Do the same in the other direction, making sixteen squares.

3. Cut apart the sixteen small squares and color each one brilliantly, both sides.

4. If you would like twenty squares, make four more from the strip of paper you cut off to make the large square.

5. Fold each small square into a triangle. Fold twice more to make a tiny triangle eight layers thick.

6. Cut a scalloped curve beginning on the layer folds. (Cut two or three snips on the long solid fold if your scissors are small and strong.)

7. Open your flowers and attach threads of different lengths.

8. Tape the other end of each thread to a rod made by rolling and taping half a sheet of paper lengthwise.

9. Tape or tie another string to the rod for hanging. If you have spread your flowers evenly, the mobile should balance properly, but if not you can add weight by sticking more tape to the lighter end.

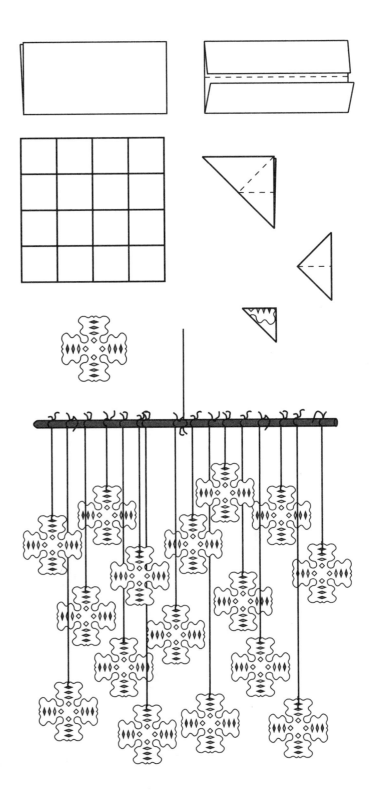

Patterns for paper caper found on page 16.

Patterns for paper capers found on pages 21 and 55.

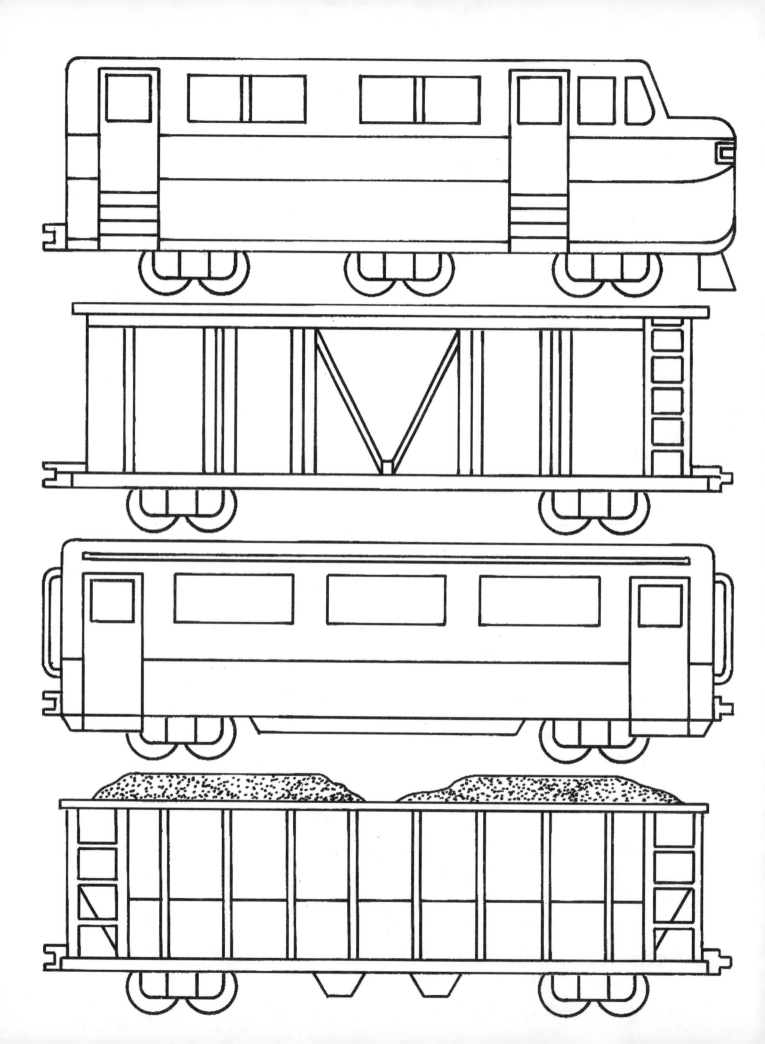

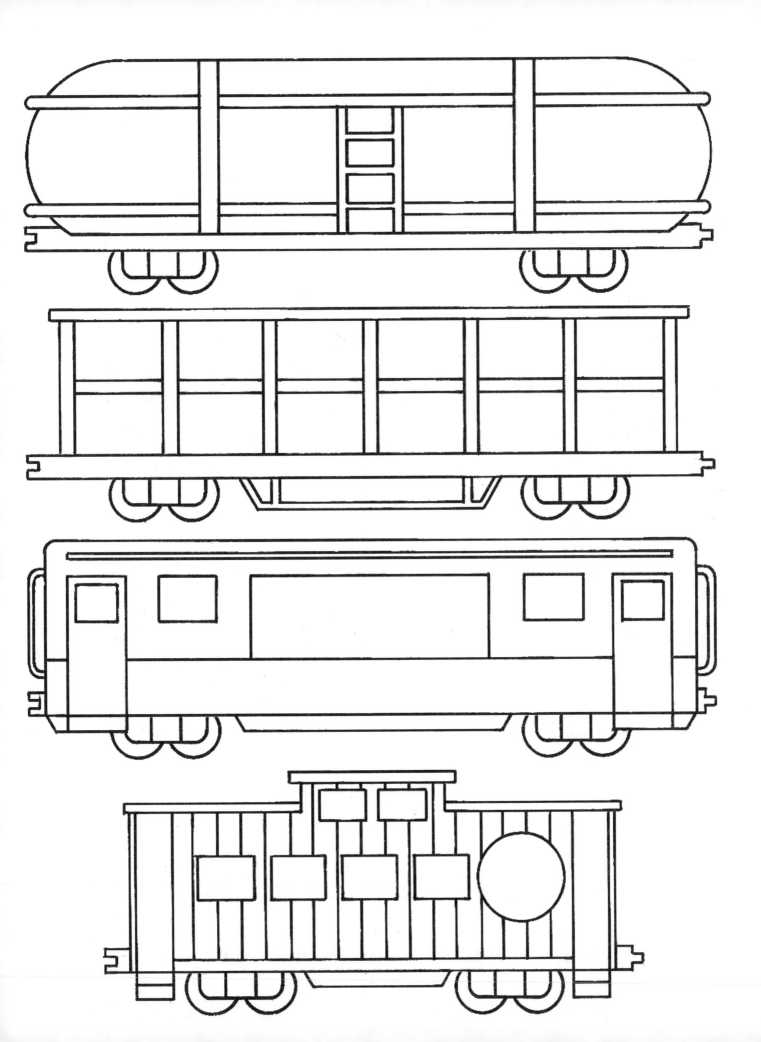

Patterns for paper caper found on page 24.

Patterns for paper caper found on page 29.

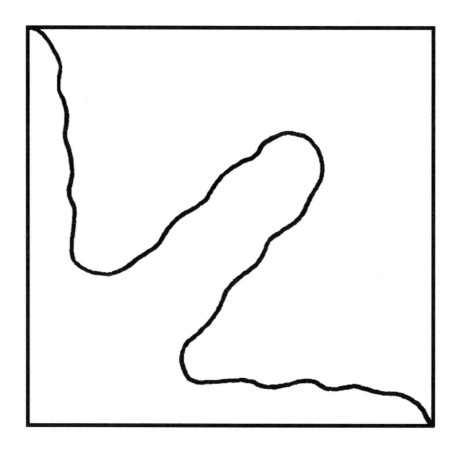

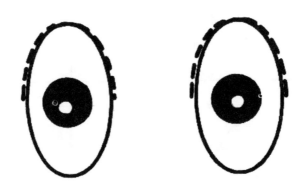

Patterns for paper caper found on page 42.

Pattern for paper caper found on page 48.

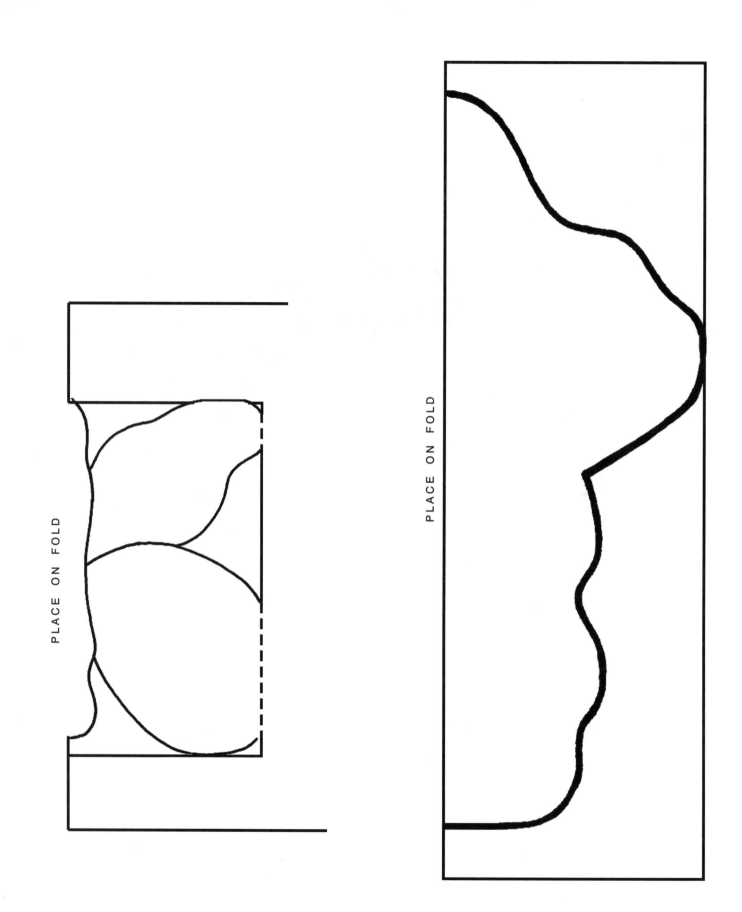

Patterns for paper capers found on pages 53 and 74.

Patterns for paper caper found on page 59.

Patterns for paper capers found on pages 19, 80, and 82.